The
LIVING
TAROT

About the Author

T. Susan Chang has been reading tarot for twenty-six years. She is the author of *Tarot Correspondences: Ancient Secrets for Everyday Readers* (Llewellyn, 2018) and *36 Secrets: A Decanic Journey through the Minor Arcana of the Tarot* (Anima Mundi, 2021), and the co-author of *Tarot Deciphered: Decoding Esoteric Symbolism in Modern Tarot* (Llewellyn, 2021). She created and hosted, with Mel Meleen, the *Fortune's Wheelhouse* esoteric tarot podcast (www.patreon .com/fortuneswheelhouse), which explores imagery and symbolism in each card of Golden Dawn–based decks like the Rider-Waite-Smith and Thoth tarots.

© Danielle Tait

She has been certified as a professional tarot reader by the American Tarot Association, offers online tarot readings and tarot mentorship sessions, and currently teaches the Living Tarot, an online tarot course for all levels of reader experience, to over 250 students. She has offered presentations and workshops at the Omega Institute, Atlas Obscura, the Northwest Tarot Symposium, StaarCon, the Philadelphia Jung Society, the Jung Society of Washington, and Tarot Singapore as well as at numerous bookstores and local tarot meetups. She is also the creator of the Arcana Case for tarot decks, which can be found at www.etsy.com/shop /tarotista, along with her line of astrological perfumes and tarot talismans, and she is a frequent podcast guest in the occult community.

Besides her work in tarot, she is the co-presenter of "Godsong: 365 Days with Homer's *Iliad* and *Odyssey*," an online course with Jack Grayle; she writes occasional cookbook reviews for NPR; and she teaches an undergraduate course on "Writing about the Senses" for Smith College. Her offerings, events, and blog posts can be found at www.tsusanchang.com. On Facebook she can be found at the Fortune's Wheelhouse Academy group; on Instagram and Twitter she is @tsusanchang.

The LIVING TAROT

Connecting the Cards to Everyday Life for Better Readings

T. SUSAN CHANG

Llewellyn Publications | Woodbury, Minnesota

FIRST EDITION
First Printing, 2023

Book design by Samantha Peterson
Cover design by Kevin R. Brown
Illustrations on pages 25, 41, 160, 161, 178–80, 204, 206, 211, and 215 by Llewellyn Art Department
Tarot Original 1909 Deck ©2021 with art created by Pamela Colman Smith and Arthur Edward Waite. Used with permission of Lo Scarabeo.

Llewellyn is a registered trademark of Llewellyn Worldwide Ltd.

Library of Congress Cataloging-in-Publication Data (Pending)
ISBN: 978-0-7387-7225-7

Llewellyn Worldwide Ltd. does not participate in, endorse, or have any authority or responsibility concerning private business transactions between our authors and the public.

All mail addressed to the author is forwarded, but the publisher cannot, unless specifically instructed by the author, give out an address or phone number.

Any internet references contained in this work are current at publication time, but the publisher cannot guarantee that a specific location will continue to be maintained. Please refer to the publisher's website for links to authors' websites and other sources.

Llewellyn Publications
A Division of Llewellyn Worldwide Ltd.
2143 Wooddale Drive
Woodbury, MN 55125-2989
www.llewellyn.com

Printed in the United States of America

Other Books by T. Susan Chang

36 Secrets
A Spoonful of Promises
Tarot Correspondences
Tarot Deciphered

FOR ALL STUDENTS
OF THE LIVING TAROT

CONTENTS

Acknowledgments

My relationship to tarot has always been that of a student—sometimes eager, sometimes truculent, often tardy. Even today, decades after I first encountered tarot, I feel like I'm wandering into an empty classroom when I draw my Cards of the Day. As the incense rises up lazily in the morning light filtering in through the windows, I consider the pen, the slip of paper, the backs of the two cards I've just drawn. Instead of the Pledge of Allegiance, I recite the Emerald Tablet of Hermes Trismegistus. "That which is below is like that which is above, and that which is above is like that which is below, to do the miracles of one only thing," I say. And then I wonder: *What will you teach me today?*

Like all good teachers, tarot is patient, generous, and meets you where you are. There are days when meaning seems to hover right out of reach, and days when it hits you with slapstick timing. There are days when you feel entirely lost and confounded, only to find the answer when you finally remember to pick up your cards. When it comes to tarot, the old saying could not be truer: when the student is ready, the teacher appears.

Tarot itself is the best of teachers. But there are many human teachers in the tarot world I am also indebted to; it's a list that would be longer than this book if I even began. So I will simply thank the two women who, I think we can all agree, are the true fairy godmothers of tarot in our time: Mary Greer and Rachel Pollack. Like so many others, I found in their books my magic beans, my enchanted pumpkin, my seven-league boots. I will always be grateful for that, and for having the great honor of their friendship today.

I am beyond grateful for having had the chance to engage with hundreds of new and experienced tarot students in the last few years—in particular, the students in the Living Tarot online course. The first Sunday of every month, when we meet over Zoom, has become a highlight of my calendar; it is fair to say I've learned as much from them as they have from me. This is also true of the Fortune's Wheelhouse Academy on Facebook, whose intrepid explorers of esoteric tarot inspire me on a daily basis.

On the publishing front, I am, as always, indebted to Llewellyn editor Barbara Moore, whose common sense, decency, and ever-open mind set the example for all gatekeepers in esoteric publishing. Nicole Borneman's eagle eye vastly improved the manuscript as it progressed through production. And I am grateful to Kat Neff and Markus Ironwood for their efforts to support and publicize my work.

Finally, I would like to thank the Fates themselves for the motion of the wheel, the spinning of the thread, and the weaving of the web.

Μοῖραι, ἀκούσατ᾽ ἐμῶν ὁσίων λοιβῶν τε καὶ εὐχῶν,
ἐρχόμεναι μύσταις λαθιπήμονες εὔφρονι βουλῇ.

INTRODUCING
THE LIVING TAROT

Today, something's different about you.

You decided to pick up a tarot deck for the first time.

Or maybe you have a tarot deck someone gave you ages ago, and for some reason it suddenly called to you.

Or maybe you've been dabbling in tarot for years, and it's never quite scratched that itch. *But you know it could.*

Whichever it is, congratulations! You bought this book, which means you've crossed a magical threshold, and when you look back at this day ten, twenty, thirty years from now, you'll say, "That was when everything changed."

But right now, let's face it: you have questions.

Any sensible person living in the twenty-first century, like you, is going to have plenty of doubts about tarot. *Is this really going to work? Am I psychic enough to do this? (I never thought I was before! What does "psychic" even mean?) What about my free will? What about fate? Can I really memorize meanings for seventy-eight cards?! Will my friends and family laugh if they find out?* And also, of course—depending on where you're coming from—*is it* evil?

THE HIGH PRIESTESS

For twenty-five years I've been reading tarot and wrestling with these questions. If I'm at peace with them today, it's because of that long journey, which was so personal and so idio-syncratic I've sometimes thought, *Can you even teach anyone tarot? Doesn't everyone have to figure it out for themselves?*

On the other hand, I don't really think that there's such a thing as a "novice tarot reader" or a "tarot beginner." I believe *anyone* can get meaningful, life-changing results from tarot from day one, because tarot is weird and uncanny and miraculous that way. So again: *Can you even teach anyone tarot?* Won't tarot happen whether you're trying or not?

Over the years, I've come to this conclusion: no, you can't teach anyone tarot. But maybe—just maybe—you can *teach someone to teach themselves tarot*, and that's what this book aims to do. Here are the two things I hope you'll come away with by the end of our time together:

1 | **Learn to find meanings in the cards for yourself.** Reading tarot, when it comes right down to it, is about finding meaning in a set of seventy-eight images. Let's face it, you're not going to learn—really learn—all those meanings from the little book that comes with the deck, or from somebody else's cookbook of meanings. They might be a starting point, but when you truly read tarot, tarot is *everywhere*; you see it, you breathe it, you feel it in your bones. That's what I mean by "living tarot."

   That's because tarot is just a way of talking about the world that exists all around you. Everything "out there" is in the cards: you just have to make the connections between tarot and the everyday life you're already living. You don't have to *memorize* the meaning of each card so much as *uncover* it.

   The good news here is: you're learning something you already know. So how hard can that be? By the end of this book (actually, by the time you've finished chapter 3), you'll have developed a core encyclopedia of seventy-eight meanings: what tarot means to you. And no one can ever take that away from you.

2 | **Figure out how tarot fits into your life.** You are a deep thinker. If you weren't, you wouldn't even be entertaining the possibility that tarot might have something to offer you. You know that looking for meaning in randomly drawn images has implications—implications about reality, about the way the world actually works.

   Chapters 4, 7, and 8 of this book offer you a way of dealing with that. They'll give you a working framework for trusting the uncanny synchronicities you deal with on a daily basis when you read tarot. I'll help you find your way to thinking about reality in a manner which, I believe, coheres and holds together intellectually. This should save you a lot of cognitive dissonance and second-guessing as you're getting going.

If you're new to tarot, this book should help you find your way to reading with a reasonable degree of fluidity and confidence by the time you get through all eight chapters. Tarot may be the work of a lifetime, but you can be up and running in a few weeks. If you've been reading tarot for a while already, this book should still help you solidify some of your practices, fill in some of your interpretive gaps, and help you find ways to crystallize and deepen your work with the cards. In fact, even after twenty-five years, I do the assignments in this book myself *all the time*—they're a core part of my praxis.

What You Need

As far as magical practices go, tarot has an incredibly low barrier to entry. You don't need an athame or a special ceremonial robe or a stack of parchment or myrrh ink. You don't need to fast for a day, or a week, or memorize any incantations. To read tarot, all you need is a set of tarot cards. And to complete this workbook, you don't need much more than that. The way I see it, there are really just three requirements if you want to undertake the work outlined in this book.

First, you'll need a Rider-Waite-Smith tarot deck. These are easy to find: look for the keywords *Rider, Waite, Smith, Pamela Colman Smith, 1909*, or any combination, like Rider-Waite or Waite-Smith. Confusing? Rider was the original publisher, Arthur Edward Waite was the magician who conceptualized it, and Pamela Colman Smith (known lovingly to tarotists everywhere as "Pixie") was the artist; the deck was first released in 1909. There are about a million different versions with different colorations, sizes, card stocks, etc. Just pick one that appeals to you and that you can imagine getting to know so well you can see it in your sleep. And yes, you can buy it for yourself in a store or online. Nobody has to give you your first tarot deck, and you don't have to steal it—please don't!

We're using Rider-Waite-Smith because it's the universal language of most English-speaking tarot readers, and because the minor arcana (Ace through 10 cards) have relatable pictures of ordinary people doing ordinary things. These are known as *scenic minors*, and not every tarot deck has them. Aleister Crowley's Thoth deck, for example, is popular for its moody, cryptic vibe, but apart from the courts and majors it contains no human figures. The Tarot de Marseille, a family of woodcut decks dating from seventeenth-century Europe (and still very popular there), has what are known as "pip cards"—featuring only the appropriate number of suit emblems on its number cards, rather like an ordinary playing card deck. In fact, many Tarot de Marseille readers work only with the major arcana. Neither Thoth nor Marseille decks will work for *The Living Tarot*, so if you're interested in those, you'll probably be better off seeking out books specifically designed for them.

The next thing that you'll need is something to write in. It really doesn't matter if it's a physical notebook or a collection of digital documents and spreadsheets. You'll be keeping track of card meanings, so if you're using a physical notebook you'll want at least one page for each of the seventy-eight cards. You'll also be doing writing exercises, word problems, filling in tables, etc. There's blank space in this workbook for you to fill out, if that's what you prefer, or you can keep your work separate on your laptop or in a special journal or in the notebook with your card meanings. If you're artistic, there will be ways for you to express that; if you're not, you won't have to. I do practically everything on my laptop, but lots of people find that writing by hand helps them remember and learn better. You do you!

The last thing you'll need is commitment. There's a lot of thinking and a lot of writing, so if you hate writing, this is probably not the workbook for you. You're also going to need to draw a Card of the Day every single day. The other assignments you can tackle on your own time—it's all right if it takes you years to read this book cover to cover—but the Card of the Day practice is something that really has to happen every day. It's not necessarily going to take you a lot of time once you're past chapter 1; you can do it in a couple minutes, or luxuriate in the process and take an hour if you want. But it needs to be part of your routine, the way brushing your teeth is part of your routine (I hope!).

If you'd like to add in some tarot content that's more esoteric, you may enjoy my other works:

- *Tarot Correspondences: Ancient Secrets for Everyday Readers* (Llewellyn, 2018): A comprehensive guide to astrological, numeric, Kabbalistic, and elemental correspondences to the cards, together with ways to use them.

- *36 Secrets: A Decanic Journey through the Minor Arcana of the Tarot* (Anima Mundi, 2021): A deep dive into the numeric (2 through 10) minor cards, and my most personal work.

- The *Fortune's Wheelhouse* podcast: A show I created with the tarot artist M. M. Meleen. It has an hour-long episode on each card, and it is available anywhere you listen to podcasts.

- *Tarot Deciphered: Decoding Esoteric Symbolism in Modern Tarot* (Llewellyn, 2021): Essentially the text version of *Fortune's Wheelhouse*, expanded out into a 600-page reference volume.

These books are not necessary for you to do the coursework. But you may find them helpful—especially for chapters 3 (Tarot Forward) and 8 (Tarot Magic). *Tarot Correspondences* in particular has a ton of reference material you might otherwise find yourself looking up online or in a variety of primary sources, which is a pain. I wrote it to save myself some trouble, and hopefully it will save you some trouble as well.

Time Frame

This is a self-directed workbook, organized into eight sections. You can take as long as you want to do them. It's not a bad idea to set goals, though, especially if you're like me and can't do anything unless there's a deadline. So here are some suggestions for how long you might take to make your way through the entirety of the work.

- **Chapter 1: Card of the Day:** One to two weeks.
- **Chapter 2: Tarot Backward:** Two to four weeks.
- **Chapter 3: Tarot Forward:** Two to four weeks.
- **Chapter 4: This I Believe:** One week.
- **Chapter 5: Ask a Question:** One to two weeks.
- **Chapter 6: Design a Spread:** Two to three weeks.
- **Chapter 7: Rituals, Ethos, Praxis:** One week.
- **Chapter 8: Tarot Magic:** Two to three weeks.

Chapters 2 and 3 are kind of twins, and you can do them simultaneously if you wish.

Don't worry if life gets the better of you and it takes you longer than the three to six months projected here. Just keep drawing a card a day, and get back to deeper study whenever you have a chance.

About the Living Tarot Online Course

The materials in this book derive from the Living Tarot online course, which I launched in 2018 and which now has over 300 students.[1] The materials are organized a little differently online, simply because of the difference between print and digital media.

If you wish, you can join the online course in addition to working through the book. If you do, you'll be able to attend the monthly Zoom meeting, where you can ask questions

---

1 | See www.tsusanchang.com/class for more information.

about the work, meet fellow students, discuss tarot synchronicities from your daily life, and try new spreads (I construct one each month). You'll also get personalized feedback on your final assignments from me. And if you make it all the way to graduation, you get to have a one-question reading with me.

Whether or not you choose to do that, I'm glad you've chosen to teach yourself to read, and more importantly, to *live* tarot. I hope your own journey with the cards is only just beginning.

one

CARD OF THE DAY

To learn tarot is to enter into a long-term relationship with meaning. And like any long-term relationship, it depends not just on the moments of high drama, tragedy, exhilaration, and romance (although these certainly occur), but on the long, quiet, peaceful, ordinary stretches of life.

Another way to look at it is this: Learning tarot is like learning a language. At first you'll only be able to use it to accomplish the most basic of needs: how to feed yourself, or how to get from one place to another (and where to find the bathroom!). But by having a little conversation every day, you gradually become comfortable communicating and picking up the subtleties, nuances, and insights that give all of our lives their texture and substance.

In this chapter, you'll learn about drawing a daily card for yourself: why and when and where and, especially, *how*. It's a habit I hope you'll keep up for life—I know I plan to. Even after a lifetime of reading tarot, I find the morning draw to be provocative, fertile, surprising, and a source of renewed hope and possibility each day.

Card of the Day provides a solid foundation for integrating tarot into the architecture of your life. It takes time, but from this praxis springs a deep capacity for metaphor. In its depths you will find an enchanted mirror, where truth endlessly shimmers if only you have the willingness and patience to look.

"Why Draw a Card Every Day?"

There are innumerable reasons to draw Card of the Day (COTD from here on out, because life is short), but here are a few of my main ones.

1 | **If you draw every day, over the course of a year, it's a virtual certainty that you will get every card.** You will never again be nervous, standing there looking at the card back and slowly turning it over—because no card will be a stranger to you. Sure, some will be close friends and some will be distant acquaintances, and some will be like relatives you barely tolerate; you may even have a crush on one or two of them! But the point is that these are facets of reality, parts of who you are. And there is no part of you that is not worth knowing.

2 | **It's good to keep promises to yourself.** As one of my favorite magical practitioners, Aidan Wachter, puts it: "I can decide to decide something once."[2] In other words, there is a freedom in not having to second-guess things in your life. You (probably) don't agonize over whether to brush your teeth each day. You probably don't engage in a few hours of soul-searching before deciding it's time for breakfast. You can take the same attitude toward tarot. Can you really keep it up every single day? Sure you can! (And if you miss a day? Just start again. Tarot will never judge you for being human.)

   Here's the thing: when you keep up a consistent daily practice, you're telling the Universe that when you make a promise to yourself, nothing is more important. And you know what? *Keeping promises to yourself is the basis of magical practice.*

3 | **Every time you shuffle a deck of cards, you invite Chance, or Fate, or Fortune to the table.** By *drawing* a card out of that chaos, you are signaling that you accept what Fate brings you through randomness. And by *interpreting* that card, you are signaling that you intend to take control of the meaning of your own fate. Because tarot is a microcosm of life, right? Life is full of uncertainties, and you never know exactly what it is going to bring you. But you can still face it, and you can take control of its meaning. Reading tarot is the micro version of that attitude, and I think you'll find it's deeply nourishing. More than that: reading tarot is a true act of courage.

4 | **COTD means discovering meanings, not memorizing them.** Now, you could go systematically through the Little White Book (LWB), like the good student you are, and try to memorize each of those little keywords: "Curiosity." "Struggle." "Distraction."

---

2 | Aidan Wachter, *Six Ways: Approaches & Entries for Practical Magic* (self-pub., Red Temple Press, 2018).

"Abundance." But those keywords, those meanings dreamed up by someone who's not you—they're so abstract! They have no connection to your personal life. Wouldn't you rather know in your bones that when you drew the 3 of Cups this morning, it was because you were going to lunch with your two friends? Wouldn't you rather know that that day you lost your keys, tarot warned you by giving you the 5 of Pentacles?

This is what it means to engage with the "Living Tarot." It means knowing—through sheer lived experience—the shape and personality of every card, the extent of its little kingdom. If you keep it up long enough, and keep track of what you drew, tarot itself will tell you what each card means. And you will never, ever forget.

5 | **If you can interpret COTD, you can interpret any card in any spread.** Learning how life shows up in the cards is literally the name of the game. If you can become fluent in the way tarot reflects life and life reflects tarot, you'll never be at a loss to derive insights from the cards for yourself or others.

"When Should I Draw My Card?"

Morning is really best. Why? because it gives your card the longest stretch of conscious, awake time to show up. It gives you the benefit of divinatory support from the moment you begin your day. So if you spill your morning coffee in your lap, or you run into a chance acquaintance while you're jogging, or there's a song you can't get out of your head while you're commuting to work, your card will give you a chance to harvest meaning from that happenstance. It will keep you company when you're alone, advise you when you're doubtful, comfort you when you're down. And when you're not thinking about it, it will just sit in the background subtly coloring your day like the strange attractor it is.

Of course, there are times when it just doesn't happen—the alarm doesn't go off, your car doesn't start, your puppy has an accident. That's all right. Don't think, *Oh well, I just won't draw today*. Do it on your lunch break, or in the waiting room at the dentist's, or on the bus. If you're nervous about carrying a deck around with you, then use a tarot app on your phone.

There is an argument for doing the draw at the *end* of the day. Some folks feel spooked by tarot's predictive power at first, and they feel more comfortable doing the draw when the day's done, as a kind of commentary on what happened. That's a way of harvesting meaning too, and if it's the only way you can handle COTD, then do that.

But do aim to draw in the morning, eventually. It's easy enough to just make it part of your routine, like brushing your teeth or shaving. By drawing in the morning, we signal that we are open to chaos. We are open to whatever happens; we are open to the randomness of this beautiful world; we are going to find ways to draw meaning from it no matter what it brings us, and we're not afraid. Trust me, it will change your life!

"How Do I Shuffle?"

Guess what? Good news! There is no wrong way to shuffle. You can do a classic riffle shuffle, which interleaves either the short end or the long end of the cards (I find it easier to shuffle the long way, since tarot cards are so much larger than playing cards). You can do the overhand shuffle, which re-orders clumps of cards as you pass them from one hand to the other. You can "smoosh" or "wash" the cards, spreading them out over a large surface and just mixing them around until they're jumbled. This last is my personal favorite—though it does lead to card reversals. We'll talk about that later.

"How Do I Choose a Card? How Many Cards Do I Draw?"

We call it Card of the Day, but Cards of the Day, plural, can also work. Personally, I draw two. Many people draw two cards because the cards can then have a kind of conversation with each other, a sort of relationship. You can try assigning roles to the cards ("Something to Look For" and "Something to Try" is a scheme I've always enjoyed). It's also nice because it increases your exposure to the full range of the deck: within six months, you'll likely have drawn all seventy-eight cards. But one card alone will give you plenty of food for thought for the day. It's really just a matter of preference.

Could you draw more? Sure. But the most important part of the practice is observing and reflecting on the draw. And personally, I find it hard to remember three cards or more as I'm going through all the distractions of my day.

Once you've shuffled, you can cut the deck, or not. You can look at the card backs while you're choosing a card, or not. You can hold a crystal or light a candle or hum to yourself, or not. And here's a secret for you doubtful types: Tarot *does not actually care* if you were not concentrating when you drew the card. Tarot doesn't care if you second-guess yourself. Tarot doesn't care if you saw a bird fly by the window and got distracted. Tarot doesn't care if you were in a bad mood when you drew the card, and tarot doesn't care if you dropped a card on the floor and had to put it back in. Tarot does not even care if you're literally not playing with a full deck—I've done that too. My point is this: go ahead and draw the card and don't be overly nervous about whether you're doing it right.

However, that said, I do have one suggestion: try using your *body* to draw the card—not just your hands. Let me explain: Some people who are very tactile, like me, may have the experience of holding the deck and feeling something quite physical. It may feel as though the deck has a sort of electric current, or a little bit of a buzz. Don't worry if you don't get that, but if you do, focus your attention on that feeling as you draw.

If that doesn't sound familiar, try this exercise, which may help you locate the "psychic buzz" in your body.

• • • • • •

Assignment 1.1
Psychic Buzz Exercise

There's a particular feeling your body experiences when you love something. Let's see if we can find it.

Instructions

1 | Think of something (or somebody) that you just adore—something that makes you feel alive, that makes your blood thrum, that makes you excited about the next time you'll encounter it. It could be a hobby, it could be a person, it could be your cat; it could be the idea of sitting down and watching Netflix after a long day. The specifics don't matter. You're looking for whatever it is that makes you feel that warm sensation. What does that feel like in your body? Imagine yourself opening up and relaxing into it. It's a good feeling, right? That's your feeling of *yes*.

Yes feels like _____ in my body.

2 | Now take a moment to think of something that you detest—something you really cannot stand. (I usually think about cheddar cheese—I know, don't hate!) You'll feel yourself physically recoiling from the thought, trying to pull yourself away from it. That's your feeling of *no*.

No feels like _____ in my body.

3 | So, now you know: the feeling of the thing you love is Yes; the feeling of the thing you hate is No. Recognize how that feels in your body: the thing that makes you kind of choke and clench versus the thing that you open yourself to. When you are drawing your card, you want to use the body to search for that feeling of Yes, of being open and relaxed and excited. This will, I promise, help you draw cards that are constructive and civic-minded, as opposed to snarky, judgmental, and/or opaque.

The metaphysics behind this notion is the idea that the cosmos runs on *eros*, on desire, like the force of gravity or the attraction of one thing for another: as above, so below. As within, so without. As you lean into that feeling connecting you to the larger patterns of the world, you reflect those patterns in your actions and all that surrounds you—including your cards.

Divination Is about Not Being Afraid

When I tell people I'm a tarot reader, there are two kinds of negative response, neither of which really bothers me. One is "Oh, I don't believe in that!" That's completely understandable. Nothing in the way we're brought up, as moderns, would make anyone predisposed to think divination has value, or that it's "real." So I don't look down on anyone who thinks this way, and I also don't have much interest in trying to make them think otherwise.

The other kind of negative response is this: "Oh, that just scares me. I don't want to know!" This is also completely understandable, but I think it's curable.

I can't emphasize this enough: *Divination is about not being afraid of what's going to happen.*

This is important because divination, at its heart, deals with the future. And the great secret gift of divination is that it enables you to face the future—whatever it may bring—with confidence and openness.

If you engage in a divinatory practice based on sortilege (random drawing from a set of meaningful objects) then you're going to get all of the cards at some point, especially if you draw a Card of the Day. If you draw one card a day, you'll probably get them all in nine months; if you draw two cards a day, you'll probably get them all in six months. My grasp of statistics is rudimentary, so I don't know why, but that's how it seems to work out.

The benefit—or maybe the drawback—of doing this is that you are going to get every card, including the scary ones. You're going to get the ones that fill you with joy and anticipation, and you're going to get the ones that make you want to roll over and go back to bed—or redo your draw. (*Don't redo your draw.* Even the cards you don't like are a gift, and the sooner you figure out the gift, the stronger your practice will be.)

Remember: there are no good or bad cards. There's only meaning. Every card has a range of light and shadow, and it can appear in any form within that range. By drawing the random card every day we're signaling that we are open to—in fact, we embrace—life's variety.

Think of it as playing a game—after all, divination is one of the Hermetic arts, and Hermes is the god of games! We engage in games with a great deal of passion—but then we let go, because it's just a game. It's the same thing when you're playing sports. You really, really care if you win at the time, and then, hopefully, you let it go. Because it's just part of life, right? You fulfill your part of life's pattern whether you win or lose, and you get to make meaning out of either outcome.

In the chaos magic movement of the 1970s, spearheaded by Austin Osman Spare, you would do a ritual or working and ask with all sincerity for the thing that you wanted. And afterward, Spare advised, you would utter the mantra "Does not matter, need not be!"[3] The theory behind this is that you want to avoid "lust of result," which I think of as the ego leaning hard on Fate to produce a precise outcome in a precise way. This is not how it works.

It's the same thing in the paradoxical headspace of divination: you're very engaged, you're very alert, but at the same time you're not pushing it. You're not trying to pressure Fate. You *care*, but you leave the details in the capable hands of Fortuna.

So to help us get into that headspace, where meaning is more important than technically "winning" or "losing," we're going to explore the idea that there are no good or bad cards. We're going to try and better understand their range of meanings: their patches of sunlight *and* their deep shadows. With time and experience, we will also become profoundly acquainted with the extensive gray areas in between.

● ● ● ● ● ●

Assignment 1.2
Too Hard! Too Easy!

It's easy to say "There are no good or bad cards," but it's a different matter entirely to stand in front of the cards, dewy-eyed with hope and anticipation, and then to draw your card, flip it over, and see…the Tower. Everything in life is in tarot, but the traditional imagery often looks more like a highlight reel—miracles! disasters! windfalls! failures!—than the relatively tame lives we actually live.

---

3 | Austin Osman Spare, *The Book of Pleasure: The Psychology of Ecstasy* (self pub., CreateSpace, 2015).

Every card has a positive side and a negative side, but some of them seem more one-dimensional than others. How do we find nuance in those very scary cards, as well as the too-good-to-be-true ones? We go hunting for it.

This exercise is intended to help you see beyond the surface of the most polarizing cards: into the benign shallows of the shadowy cards, and into the murky depths of the bright and cheery ones. It's meant to help you not freak out the first time you draw the 10 of Swords as your Card of the Day. It's also meant to inoculate against disappointment the day you draw the 10 of Cups and you don't actually meet your soul mate.

Instructions

I'll call the more daunting cards "Dark Side" cards (I've chosen the 10 of Swords, the Devil, the Tower, 5 of Pentacles, 3 of Swords, 9 of Swords, and 5 of Cups). The deceptively light-filled ones are called "Bright Side" cards (the Sun, 10 of Pentacles, 4 of Wands, 3 of Cups, 9 of Cups, 10 of Cups, and the aces). The assignment is pretty simple: For the Dark Side cards, think of some positive ways of interpreting the card. For the Bright Side cards, think of some negative ways of interpreting the card. Grab a notebook or your tarot journal and go to town! I've provided some leading questions for each as prompts.

The Dark Side

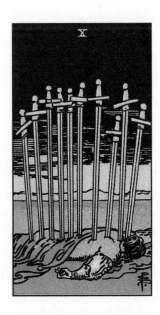

10 of Swords: Why's there light on the horizon? Where's the blood? If the swords are thoughts, what happens next?

Death by a thousand cuts - bloodless but actual

All seems lost but there's light on the horizon

The Devil: What are the Devil's skills and talents? Why is he so tempting? Why are the people so loosely bound?

_____

_____

_____

_____

_____

_____

The Tower: What is the purpose of thunder and lightning? How does the atmosphere feel beforehand and afterward?

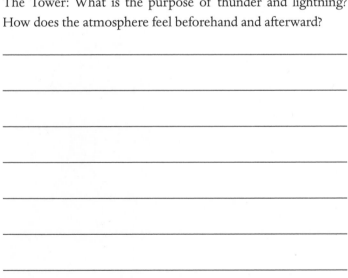

_____

_____

_____

_____

_____

_____

5 of Pentacles: Are the people leaving, going into, or unaware of the church? Whose job is it to help them?

_____

_____

_____

_____

_____

_____

3 of Swords: How do you feel before and after a "big cry"? How can changing your thoughts (Swords) affect your heart? If ignorance equals bliss, what equals sadness?

_____

_____

_____

_____

_____

_____

_____

9 of Swords: How do you feel when you wake up from a nightmare? Which way are the swords pointing? What do you see on the blanket? What function does a blanket serve?

_____

_____

_____

_____

_____

5 of Cups: What is the bridge for? Why are two of the cups standing? What should the mournful figure do with them?

_____

_____

_____

_____

_____

The Bright Side

The Sun: What happens if there's too much sun? Too much heat and light? What risks come with overconfidence?

_____

_____

_____

_____

_____

_____

10 of Pentacles: Everything's safe and established. But what if you want to move? Have an adventure? Take a risk?

_____

_____

_____

_____

_____

_____

4 of Wands: Cut flowers don't last—what's after the party? What's the difference between short-term pleasure and long-term happiness?

_____

_____

_____

_____

_____

_____

3 of Cups: Ever tripped while dancing? Why? Seasonal celebrations are great—what comes after the harvest?

_____

_____

_____

_____

_____

_____

9 of Cups: What's under that drape? What's the difference between image and real life? What does the "man who has everything" miss out on?

_____

_____

_____

_____

_____

_____

_____

10 of Cups: Does "happily ever after" equal real life? What happens after you take a bow? Why is the couple's back turned to us?

_____

_____

_____

_____

_____

_____

Ace of Wands, Cups, Swords, Pentacles: Aces are opportunities. Ever missed an opportunity? Why?

_____

_____

_____

Deconstructing the Tower

Eventually, if you draw your Card of the Day faithfully, the card will *tell you* what it means: how it can be subtle, or shy, or underhanded, or exaggerated. It will give you a comprehensive tour of its gray areas, which will slowly come into view.

The Tower has a reputation for being the most stressful card in tarot. But remember, every card has a range of meanings from the positive to the negative. I'm going to share with you some of the ways the Tower has shown up for me, over the fifty-eight recorded times (as of this writing) that I've drawn it.

- **Thunderstorms.** You can see that this is probably the best card tarot has to represent lightning and thunder.
- **Physical obstacles.** One time I was driving along and I couldn't get to the place I wanted to get to because the bridge was closed. It had collapsed; it had fallen apart; it had been demolished by a natural event.

- **Mundane context.** I had to travel to New York for an event. I don't like to see the Tower when I'm traveling, but you know, you take what you get and you don't get upset. Well, it turned out—and I only realized this halfway through the day—that the day that I went to New York was the anniversary of September 11, which was very much a Tower occurrence, wasn't it? So, you know, sobering…but not necessarily personally disastrous for me on that day. Just something to remember that affected me.

- **Minor accidents.** For example, one day, I spilled rice all over the counter. Quite recently, I was cooking next to the stove with the burner on and the wrapping for the meat I was cutting was too close to the flame of the burner and caught on fire. No big deal—the smoke alarms went off, I dumped the wrapping in the sink, and I doused it with water.

- **Tripping and spilling stuff.** I've drawn the Tower on a day I dropped a plate and broke it, including the time my daughter dropped an entire stack of plates!

- **Other people's problems.** I've seen it in a reading for a client who had catastrophic fire damage to their house.

- **Resounding defeats.** Once my son, who is a sort of professional-level fencer, was demolished in his first bout.

- **Content.** I drew it the day I listened to, as it happened, a podcast on spontaneous human combustion.

One of my absolute favorite manifestations of the Tower happened on a day when I was walking out in the woods, and I found a beer bottle that was just lying there on our property. (We have about sixteen acres, so people are walking through there all the time.) The bottle was still sealed. I picked it up and thought, *Well, here's a Tower thing I can do.* I pried the cap off the bottle using a handy rock, and I poured it out as a libation, turning it upside down the way the people in the image are falling upside down. It was a way of honoring the spirit of the card and fulfilling its message.

We'll talk more about that kind of thing, which is actually a form of sympathetic magic, in chapter 8. But my point is that you must look for the cards—even the hard ones—to show up in ways that are interesting, creative, different, sometimes easily overlooked, even humorous. One of the things I like to say is: *it's worth delighting in even the smallest of Fortune's children.*

Of course, there's going to be a time when you get the Tower and you really do have a terrible day. And you know what? You're not going to be sad that the Tower showed up. You're not going to think the Tower caused your day to be terrible. You're going to realize that the

Tower *validates your experience*. Tarot understands that you've had a shitty day and it's saying that, in the only language that it has: "Yeah, your day sucked! I feel your pain!" And you'll think, *It's nice that somebody understands.* My point is, you don't have to feel bad about feeling real things.

One final point: even on the worst day, there's always a better and a worse response. In other words: For any given card—be it the Tower or anything else—a range of better and worse outcomes is possible. Which one of them shows up depends, to at least some degree, on your own actions. When you engage thoughtfully with every single card, it's a way of recognizing that you're going to choose the better way.

And that's one more reason I think everyone should read tarot: you learn that, on some level, you get to choose how you receive what's happening in your world. That's a good thing.

Reflecting on Your COTD

You've figured out how and when you're going to shuffle and draw. You've mentally prepared yourself to draw any card whatsoever. Now let's talk about how to start a conversation with that card. Drawing it is only the beginning!

Once you've drawn your COTD, it's a good idea to snap a picture of the draw with your phone so you can have it with you all day. (You could also just carry the card around with you, but if you're like me, that raises any number of complications, from spilled coffee to curious coworkers to actually misplacing it on the subway.) Because what really gives the COTD practice its traction in your life is what you do with it afterwards, in the mundane, everyday hours that follow. By hunting for the way the card shows up during the day—its *epiphanies*—you build it into your life. Not just at the moments of high drama, like when you got married or you moved into your first apartment or you retired. Every single day, tarot invites us to layer added meaning and context onto what we see all around us in ordinary life.

Human beings are volatile. During the course of an ordinary day, we go through an extraordinary range of moods and perspectives. Sometimes we're hopeful, sometimes we're resigned, sometimes we're curious or resentful or giddy. In any given day, there are many inflection points, and some of them are perfect opportunities to reflect on your card. Here's a few of them:

• When you're doubtful

• When you're upset

- When you're in between tasks
- When you're confused
- When something exciting just happened
- When you're kind of just…buffering

At moments like these, where you're adrift on the sea of your day, it's good to ask your card for its perspective; a kind of second opinion. In an ideal world, tarot acts as something like a best friend—or, maybe, the best version of yourself: happy, secure, and capable. Because your true Self contains many selves, and at least one of them has something relevant and supportive to offer you at all times. The best version of yourself is never at a loss for advice, or support, or companionship and conversation. In other words, tarot is a reminder that you never need to feel alone.

Finally: if you, like me, have a tendency to get so caught up in your day you forget to think about your card at all, you can also set an alarm to go off at random times of day to prompt you to think about it.

Layers of Meaning: Five Ways into a Tarot Card

When you're checking in with your card over the course of the day, you're undoubtedly going to wonder, *How do I even begin to make sense of this image? How do I start connecting it to what's going on with me right now?* You might take a look at the card and—nothing. Don't worry; this happens to everyone. What I'm going to offer you is a way of approaching that image systematically, layer by layer, and burrowing your way into it until you hit pay dirt.

Layer 1: Visual

The first and most obvious way into a tarot card: what you see is what you get. Look at the visual imagery of the card. Don't even think about what it might symbolize; just look at the picture.

If you're looking at the 3 of Pentacles, you might look around and ask: Am I seeing anything that looks like this? Am I seeing three people in a room talking to each other? Am I in a building that has architectural elements that kind of look like this? Is there a bench in the room, and do I need to stand on it to get that book that's high up on my bookshelf?

And here's a pro tip for working visually with tarot cards, especially the number cards: *tarot likes to count.* See those three pentacles carved in the arch? Be on the lookout for them. You might discover three coins in your pocket. You might walk past a pawn shop, because

the ancient symbol for a pawn shop was three brass balls in a triangle configuration. You can sometimes see that symbol hanging outside or on a painted sign. Or you might eat three cookies. (In fact, I wouldn't hold it against you if you ate three cookies *on purpose* after drawing this card. See chapter 8.)

Layer 2: Mood

What's the mood or feeling in your card? Different people will see different things (and that's the beauty of tarot). What I see in the 3 of Pentacles is this: three people who are studiously engaged in something or trying to plan something. Maybe they're collaborating or making an effort to act collegial with one another.

Over the course of your day, there's a very good chance you'll encounter this feeling, even if it doesn't look exactly like the image on the card. If you work in an office, for example, you might be talking to your coworkers by the coffee machine or during a meeting. You might be trying to work something out with the marketing department, or making a series of phone calls, or setting up appointments.

If you're not in an office (and fewer and fewer of us are these days), it could be that you're talking to someone on Zoom or sending an important email to collaborate on a project. *It doesn't have to look like the card to feel like the card*, is my point.

Layer 3: Other People

The visual or emotional information in the card doesn't have to happen to you personally. It could be something that you witness happening to someone else. For example, you might walk past the conference room and see three people having a meeting. You might pass a cafe and catch sight of three plates at a table setting or three people enjoying their lunch together. In fact, as we speak, I'm looking out the window into my neighbor's yard, where three men and a backhoe are currently digging a new septic system. They're not angry or idle or excited or restless; they're just doing their job. That's classic 3 of Pentacles.

Layer 4: Body Language

The beautiful thing about tarot decks like Rider-Waite-Smith that show lots of people doing lots of things is that they're just full of gestures and poses and physical attitudes. You'll notice, if you adopt the posture of a tarot character, that just doing that gives you a ton of information about what they might be experiencing internally. (Try it!)

In the case of the 3 of Pentacles, we've got three figures, each in a different physical posture. See the one on the right, with the fantastic polka-dot hooded cape? Maybe you run across someone holding forth something they want to draw your attention to—a book or a newspaper or a map, say. Or maybe you're doing that yourself. Or you might notice someone looking at you (or someone else) with an extremely attentive air, like the tonsured monk standing by the central pillar. It could be that you're hammering something or drawing something like the artisan on the bench. You could be designing something, or teaching someone, or even cooking something, and find yourself in that industrious pose.

Layer 5: Content!

This last point is important, and frequently overlooked. I'm willing to bet that over the course of a day, you consume a ton of content: books, games, social media, podcasts, TikToks, Netflix. All day long you're taking content into your head. You could be reading a Twitter thread about a debate three people had, or watching a TED talk about whether or not we actually live in three dimensions. You could be watching a series on Amazon Prime and notice three people in a living room talking about their latest crisis, and that could be your 3 of Pentacles too.

I'll tell you a secret: *tarot does not distinguish between the inner and outer worlds*. If it happened in your mind and never occurred in the external world at all? As far as tarot is concerned, that's just as real as something that happened in front of your actual face or in your actual house. The same goes for dreams—including daydreams.

Ultimately, you may well find layers that go beyond these; for example, esoteric correspondences. After learning the correspondences, you might find yourself saying "Oh, well this is related to Mars in Capricorn, in the second decan, and Mars is exalted in Capricorn. And it's related to the sephira Binah on the Tree of Life in Kabbalah, which means that it's also related to all the Queens of tarot." At that point, you've got everything you associate with all those concepts—Mars, Capricorn, exaltation, Binah, Queens—that you can add in, if you like. The neural network you can build up from your explorations is infinite!

My point is that it pays to be very broad-minded about your card of the day and to look for it in ways that may seem quite subtle. Tarot is not always going to hit you over the head, and that's a good thing, because as human beings we really can't deal with drama 24/7. By looking for connections with your card in this way, you are teaching yourself to live as if you're in a poem or a work of art. By keeping an eye open for these tiny synchronicities, you start to get the sense that reality is fractal; tiny patterns reflect bigger ones, and the tiny ones are no less perfect and intricate than the bigger ones. You are the kaleidoscope—and the glass chips, and the mirror, and the pattern that arises from them. All of it.

In short, there's no right way or a wrong way to read a card. There's only meaning, and that's what we're looking for. Our lives are, quite literally, meaningful.

"Yeah, But What's My Card Trying to Say?"

What is the purpose of a tarot deck? If you ask most people who don't read tarot (or many who do, for that matter) the answers will likely fall into one of these broad categories:

- **Description (or "Prediction"):** The card offers you a glimpse of what's going to happen during your day, or what's going to show up in your world. It's like an ambassador from the nation-state of Destiny; a representative of Fate. Whatever message it's delivering, you don't get a choice about it. Depending on how extreme your views on fate are, that could mean anything from "I'm going to meet a tall, dark, and handsome stranger" to "There will be a prize in my cereal" to "I'm going to be in an accident—oh no!"

- **Prescription (or "Advice"):** The card tells you what you should or should not do. Like a helicopter parent or an interfering aunt, it provides warnings, admonitions, and exhortations. It is a tireless dispenser of advice and pro tips, and you ignore these at your peril. In the model scenario, you respond to and perform each of these prompts faultlessly throughout the whole day.

I think there's a problem with both of these attitudes, the descriptive and the prescriptive. If you subscribe to the descriptive or "predictive" view, you run the danger of becoming ensnared in fatalism. And the danger of *that* is that you become a kind of cog in the machine of your own life, an automaton hijacked by your own belief in your own predestination.

And if you subscribe to the prescriptive or "advice" view, you're giving up your agency in a different way, a reactive way. Are you really not going to go on that bike ride on this beautiful day because you drew the Tower? You don't need tarot to tell you what to do. Chances are you already have plenty of people who tell you what to do. Your boss tells you what to do. Your god tells you what to do. Your mom tells you what to do. For heaven's sake, just have this one area of your life where no one tells you what to do!

Here's what I suggest: instead of considering your card draw as either a prescription or a description, consider it an *invitation*. The card does not have to tell you what's going to happen or what you ought to do (though elements of both may arise). In the best case, as we've said, it stands in for the best version of yourself. But since the best version of yourself may not always be available, you can think of your card as a kind of tour guide. It points out areas of particular relevance or interest; sometimes it has a lot to say, and sometimes it's rather quiet. It invites you to contemplate something and consider its significance. It invites you to consider the best and worst aspects of a given situation and how to respond. It's an emphasizer. You are not bound to its suggestions, though there is no harm in paying attention to them.

Card of the Day is an invitation to harvest meaning from your card. It's an invitation to be in conversation with Fate, to become a magnet for synchronicity and coincidence. It's an invitation to discover your own sense of being engaged in and part of larger patterns in this world. And you don't need the card to tell you what to do in order to feel the beauty and the power of that, right?

Assignment 1.3

Card of the Day Checklist

Okay! Having mentally prepared yourself for virtually any cartomantic appearance, no matter how dramatic, you're ready to get started with your COTD practice. Rejoice! For today is the beginning of the rest of your life!

Here's the framework—and remember, the card is a metaphor. Be very, very open-minded.

1. Draw

- Note the date.
- Draw using any shuffling technique you care to.
- Note the card.
- Note the deck, if you're the kind of person who uses lots of different decks.
- Take a picture of the card with your phone for easy reference.

Using whatever you can sense/find out about the card, from its appearance, its mood, its body language, imagery, keyword, or correspondences:

- What could be the positive message of the card?
- What could be the negative message of the card?
- Looking ahead at your day, think of five to ten things that might happen today, and list them. These do not have to have any apparent connection to the card (though a connection may make itself plain later on!).

2. Observe

Throughout the day, look for scenes, moments, or ideas that match up with your card. These could be:

- Visual rhymes
- Feelings/moods
- Other people
- Gestures/body language
- Content references—movies, books, radio, podcasts, videos, etc.

Card of the Day Checklist

Date:_____

1. Draw

The card(s) I drew today: _____

Take a picture of the card with your phone for easy reference.
Using whatever you can sense/find out about the card, from its appearance, its keyword, or correspondence tables:

What could be the positive message of the card?

_____

What could be the negative message of the card?

_____

Looking ahead to your day, think of five to ten things that might happen today and list them here.

_____

_____

_____

_____

2. Observe

Throughout the day, look for scenes, moments, ideas that match up with your card. These could be: visual rhymes, feelings/moods, other people, gestures/body language, content references: movies, books, radio, podcasts, videos.

_____

_____

_____

_____

3. Dialogue

During the day, you will experience moments where you're excited, concerned, in limbo, uncertain how to proceed. These are perfect times to check in and have a conversation with the card.

What is it saying? Is its positive or negative message helpful to you?

_____

_____

4. End-of-Day Look Back

At the end of the day, consider: What were some significant things that happened today? ("significant" can mean: emotionally significant, captured your attention, or simply took up a big portion of your day). Do any of those seem to connect to the card?
(Example: *Made a decision about a new car. VII Chariot = car.*)

_____

_____

_____

_____

_____

_____

_____

Log any meanings that seem especially significant in your Card Meanings journal.

Congratulations! Even if you only get two or three hits, you've signaled to your tarot practice that you're open for business. Keep it up!

3. Dialogue

During the day, you will experience moments where you're excited, concerned, in limbo, uncertain how to proceed, or just "in neutral." These are perfect times to check in and have a conversation with the card.

- What is it saying? Is its positive or negative message helpful to you?

4. End-of-Day Look Back

At the end of the day, consider:

- What were some significant things that happened today? ("Significant" can mean moments that were emotionally significant, captured your attention, or simply took up a big portion of your day.)
- Do any of those seem to connect to the card? How? (Example: Made a decision about a new car. The Chariot = car.)
- Log any meanings that seem especially significant in your Card Meanings journal.

Congratulations! Even if you only got two or three hits, you've signaled to your tarot practice that you're open for business. Keep it up!

Chapter 1 Final Assignment
Ten Synchronicities

Now that you're learning to spot the "meaningful coincidences" between tarot and ordinary life, let's celebrate them!

Instructions

Use the Card of the Day checklist for a couple of weeks running. Then find your ten best matches, where the card seemed to speak *directly* to something in your day, whether it was an everyday event that happened to you, something you observed, or something you merely found yourself thinking about. Name the card and explain in a sentence or two what the connection was. If you like, take a picture to remind you how you made the connection.

Examples

- Ace of Pentacles reversed: *My laptop's On button started malfunctioning!*
- 5 of Pentacles: *Heard a story about family separation policy on the news. The pool was locked when I went for my swim—no workout today!*
- 4 of Wands: *My birthday! Went shopping and celebrated with my spouse.*
- 5 of Cups: *Five eggs broke when I dropped the container.*
- King of Wands: *Finally made up my mind and bought an electric blanket! (Wands = fire = heat)*
- 3 of Swords: *It rained all day today. (Rain on 3 of Swords card)*
- The Moon: *Big, beautiful, bright full moon in the sky tonight! Went to sleep early and had crazy dreams.*
- Ace of Cups: *Set up drip irrigation in my garden.*
- 10 of Swords: *My friend Alan told me about the Japanese tradition of* Hari-Kuyō, *or "needle mass" (funeral for broken needles!), which happens to fall on this date.*
- 8 of Wands: *Got my bike running and went for a spin!*
- Knight of Cups: *Our friend Mike crossed the river and came for dinner and told a lot of stories.*

• Death: *Death with his scythe was me with my cultivator, planting "heads" of garlic. Also, I associate Death with compost and weekend chores. Also, we're in Scorpio, and garlic is always planted in Scorpio season. Also, I associate Mars with garlic, and Mars rules Scorpio. Also, it's the thirteenth today!* [4]

_____

_____

_____

_____

_____

_____

_____

_____

_____

_____

_____

4 | This last one is a rather extreme example of using astrological correspondences. The Death card is associated with the zodiacal sign of Scorpio in the Golden Dawn tradition. For much, much more of this, see my book *Tarot Correspondences*.

One Last Thing Before You Move On to Chapter 2

The information you record is a gold mine, and you ought to treat it as such. That means *don't stop* and *keep a record*.

What do you mean, don't stop?! After you complete this final assignment, continue to record your draws in whatever way is most sustainable for you. It's enough to note down what card(s) you drew and a sentence (or even just a few words) describing what matched. If you have the energy, it's also a good idea to note anything big that happened that *didn't* seem to match—because chances are, someday you'll see it actually did.

What do you mean, keep a record?! Personally, I find the easiest way to ensure I track my draws is to keep them in an Excel spreadsheet. I can't lose it, and besides entering the day's data and the spell I write for the draw (see chapter 8), I have all sorts of algorithms running inside the spreadsheet that tabulate card frequencies, astrological correspondences, number correspondences, etc.

You may well prefer an analog method, like sitting down with a glass of wine at the end of the day and writing mindfully with a fountain pen in a beautiful leather-bound journal with acid-free gilt-edged parchment pages. If that's your deal, fantastic; you're a lot classier than I am! Just make sure you don't give up on it when you go on that big overseas trip and you're trying to avoid the luggage surcharge and you're thinking, *Do I really need to take this with me?* The answer is *Yes, you do*. So make sure your method of recording is something that's not too annoying or bulky or embarrassing to take anywhere and everywhere. Because this is how you build your language and your understanding and your private idiom with the deck. And I promise you, if you keep it up, it will happen, as surely as night follows day.

two
TAROT BACKWARD

In the first chapter of this book, we learned the Card of the Day practice, which I hope will be with you for the rest of your days as a reader. In fact, you could do *only* Card of the Day for the rest of your life, never trying another spread or reading for anyone else, and you could still legitimately call yourself a tarot reader. But in order to make this practice deep enough and meaningful enough that you're going to want to stick with it, you'll need this chapter and the next one. I call them "Tarot Backward" and "Tarot Forward."

"Tarot Backward" and "Tarot Forward" are the beating heart of the Living Tarot. They are the DNA, the neural network, the critical infrastructure of your relationship to tarot, and I encourage you to take as long as you need with them. In fact, these skills and exercises are so fundamental that I do them myself *all the time*—even now, decades into my life as a tarot reader—just to keep practicing and remain fluent and flexible in their application.

Tarot Backward: The World Is Your Filing Cabinet

Here's a typical portrait of life as a new tarot reader: You start by reading the Little White Book that comes with the book, understandably enough. You look up meanings online, or maybe if you're savvy you get one of the classic tarot texts, like Rachel Pollack's *Seventy-Eight Degrees of Wisdom* or Mary Greer's *Tarot for Your Self;* maybe you even pick up one of my own books, like *Tarot Correspondences* or *Tarot Deciphered.* You start vacuuming up definitions, meanings, and correspondences. And then, good student that you are, you try to memorize them.

Not long thereafter, this starts to drive you a bit crazy, for a couple of different reasons:

1 | *Memorizing is hard.* It uses that analytical left side of the brain. Even if you have a highly developed left brain, that doesn't mean it's easy to internalize things that you have no connection to other than brute memorization. For a brain that's evolved to handle a maximum of seven things at a time, seventy-eight is just a big number. It's no wonder folks often get discouraged or even give up trying to learn tarot because it's just too hard to load up seventy-eight meanings in your brain.

2 | *Memorizing is the opposite of intuiting.* The harder you work at memorizing, the more you end up shutting down your Spidey sense. Suppose your friend comes to you feeling depressed and you draw the 5 of Pentacles for them. If you're concentrating on what Mercury ruling the first decan of Taurus has to do with that card, you might miss the fact that it's simply saying they're flat broke, or socially bankrupt, or just feeling lonely.

But here's the thing (and the reason why you really don't have to memorize at all): everything in life—from tying your shoelace to falling in love to bumping into someone on the subway or watching cat videos—is in tarot.

If you're trying to memorize meanings, your train of thought may go something like this: *My LWB says that Temperance, and the 2 of Pentacles, and the 2 of Swords, and Justice, and the World, all might mean "balance." Okay, what does balance look like in my life? It's me juggling work-life priorities. It's me literally trying to learn to ride this bike, or ice skating for the first time. It's me eating healthy. It's me having good boundaries.*

Before you know it, everything and nothing starts to sound like "balance." And how do you even know which kind of balance goes with which card? But if you start from the specific example itself it's another story. Suppose you've just gone through a divorce and the judge has finally ruled on your child support arrangement. Of course it's not a happy situation, but you know it's fair and you're glad you're done with that process. You look at your tarot deck and in this case—it's obvious to you!—Justice is the card that speaks to you.

Here's another couple of examples: You probably have had a broken heart at one time or another, I'm sorry to say. If you've experienced that kind of sorrow, it's not hard for you to recognize it when you look at the 3 of Swords (whose Hermetic title is actually the "Lord of Sorrow"). *Ah, I know that card,* you think ruefully. In the same way, you've probably enjoyed being out with friends eating and drinking. It's easy to look around you when you're out carousing and think, *This is like the 3 of Cups.*

Unlike the thousands of concrete events that make up our lives, a tarot card is fuzzy around the edges. It resists specification. Imagine you work at the supermarket and I ask you where I can find something that is "filling." You don't know if I mean pizza, or a steak, or a loaf of sourdough, or three-bean dip. We end up staring at each other, getting increasingly frustrated. But if I ask you where I can find a potato, you know exactly where that is and you can point me to aisle two in Produce in no time flat.

In other words, it's a whole hell of a lot easier to start with what you know. Because tarot is simply a way of describing everything in life that you're already familiar with—all the things that you were born with; everything that's gone into making you the terrific person you are today. What we do in "Tarot Backward"—and I'm certainly not the first tarot reader or teacher to use this technique—is look at the world around us. We find some common things all of us experience in our everyday lives, and we figure out which tarot cards they go with.

Since there's only seventy-eight cards, it's always true that every card is going to have many, many meanings. (And it's sometimes also true that two different cards can mean the same thing. Just as we have synonyms in language, there are synonyms across the deck.) But by working backward from the things you know, you're developing a language. You're developing a way of thinking about the world metaphorically that will allow you to translate anything you see into tarot—and then from tarot back into your real life.

Backward versus Forward Tarot: You Are the Mapmaker

Systematic thinking and memorization aren't all bad. I think in each of us there's a little (or a lot of) left-brain capacity, and tarot can make use of that. And this is where correspondences come in.

Correspondences (for example: the Hermit corresponds to the sign of Virgo; minor cards numbered 5 correspond to ordeals) are what I like to call *Forward Tarot*. Forward Tarot is like a scaffolding; an outline; a neural network of associated concepts. It allows you to project, to fill in the gaps for those parts of your life that don't obviously seem to join up with a tarot card.

By using correspondences, you create a web of meanings, a system for connecting the dots so that you can find what it is in your life that joins up symbolically, metaphorically, or figuratively with a tarot card. Forward Tarot stretches the scope of every tarot card so that more can fit in it. It's sort of like a map that way; a map allows you to go places you have never been. You may have never been to the Arctic, but you know if you just keep traveling north, you'll get there. Correspondences are like that: they give you the tools you need to stretch beyond what you already know.

Backward Tarot is a right-brain kind of thing, where you intuitively grasp the nature of what you're thinking about and simply assign it to a card. Forward Tarot is a way of projecting out and building systems so you'll be able to find more of those connections and tie them back into the cards. You can certainly use the correspondence systems we inherited from the Golden Dawn through the Rider-Waite-Smith tarot. But I encourage you to also try and make up some correspondences of your own, because they'll stick better. Backward Tarot provides content; Forward Tarot provides structure—that's why you really need both.

If you want to use a language-learning analogy, Backward Tarot is like teaching somebody a language that you already know. If somebody asks you the rules for when you should say the word "for" versus the word "to" or the word "toward," you'd probably kind of say them in your head to see how you use them and then come up with a rule. That's like Backward Tarot. Whereas if you are *learning* a language from scratch, you might at some point have to consult a table or chart that provides a grammatical structure for you, and you memorize those rules until they're internalized. That's Forward Tarot, and we'll talk about it in chapter 3.

Chapter 2 Assignments: An Overview

You're going to be doing eight different assignments in this chapter: two for the major arcana, two for the minor arcana, two for the courts, one for the four suits generally, and then a final assignment using what you've learned.

Each of these assignments contains a set of vocabulary, a set of ideas describing the human experience. Each of them gives you a limited set of tarot cards to match up with those experiences. I've included both *internal* types of experiences and *external* types of experience. For example, *internally* the Emperor might represent the sensation of decisiveness. But on the other hand, he could also represent bosses you've had, or your father, or the president—all of which are *external*. (Unless you happen to be the president, I guess, in which case, I'm honored, but I think you should stop reading this book and get back to the infrastructure bill.)

Don't worry if the cards that you come up with don't seem to quite fit the concepts exactly. You might also find you have more than one card for each concept, or more than one concept for each card. As I've said before, the deck is full of synonyms in just the same way our language is full of synonyms—it's not a one-to-one thing. For example, the experience of being alone could be the 5 of Pentacles, but it could also be the Hermit, or the Queen of Swords.

While it could show up in many different cards, it's not going to show in *every* card; I very much doubt you'll find the experience of being alone in the 3 of Cups.

The point of these exercises is to start drawing connections and build up the language on your own. And this process never ends, even when you've been reading tarot for a bunch of years. Suppose one day you find yourself having a new experience: Let's say you're on TV for the first time. When you have a moment to collect yourself, you'll ask yourself, *What card could this be?* And after you think about it for a couple minutes, you'll realize it's a card that's related to fame (say, 6 of Wands), or expertise (say, the Hermit), or feeling self-conscious (say, the Moon), or being popular (say, 3 of Cups), depending on how the moment is landing with you.

As you work through these assignments, you'll want to add the meanings you collect into whatever journal or binder or spreadsheet you've chosen to use. Suppose you matched up loneliness with the Hermit—you'll go to the Hermit page (or entry) and you'll jot down "loneliness." This is how you'll build up your warehouse of meanings for every card, until each is surrounded by what Jung called a "diffuse cloud of cognition."[5]

On the previous page is a "cloud of cognition" I use for the High Priestess.

One final note before you dive in: The human experience is, of course, infinite, but this book is not. The concepts and terms I've introduced in these assignments are just the beginning. If you want to add in your own as you work your way through them, please feel free to do so.

• • • • • •

Assignment 2.1

Major Arcana: The Building Blocks of Personhood

As we progress through Tarot Backward, we're going to try and find both internal and external meanings. In the case of the major arcana, I'm calling the internal meanings "Building Blocks of Personhood." These are universal character aspects; for example, perseverance or self-discipline or patience or curiosity.

Instructions

1 | Spread out all twenty-two major arcana in front of you.

2 | Have a look at this list of internal qualities and characteristics. Think about each one and look to see which card reminds you of that quality. Jot it down in the attached chart. There are no right or wrong answers.

3 | Add other qualities/characteristics you think of to the list. Try to stick to basic elements of character rather than passing moods like frustration or nervousness or satisfaction (those we'll cover more in the minor arcana).

integrity	self-discipline	altruism	obsession	perseverance
imagination/vision	patience	leadership/decisiveness	open-mindedness
creativity	aspiration	self-knowledge	endurance	objectivity/fairness
flexibility	self-regulation	tradition/received principles	free will/choice
hope	introspection	resilience	articulation	force
logic/reasoning	resourcefulness	intuition	knowledge

---

5 | C. G. Jung, *Memories, Dreams, Reflections* (New York: Random House, 1965), 308.

THE FOOL.

THE MAGICIAN.

THE HIGH PRIESTESS

THE EMPRESS.

THE EMPEROR.

THE HIEROPHANT

_____   _____   _____   _____   _____   _____

THE LOVERS.

THE CHARIOT.

STRENGTH.

THE HERMIT.

WHEEL of FORTUNE

JUSTICE .

_____   _____   _____   _____   _____   _____

THE HANGED MAN.

DEATH.

TEMPERANCE.

THE DEVIL.

THE TOWER.

THE STAR.

_____   _____   _____   _____   _____   _____

THE MOON.

THE SUN.

JUDGEMENT.

THE WORLD.

_____   _____   _____   _____

Assignment 2.2

Major Arcana Backward: Trends

While courage or strength or perseverance might be internal qualities, the "Trends" assignment focuses on things that happen to you, which you experience as outside of yourself: initiations, endings, course corrections, or accidents.

change	smooth sailing	crisis	uncertain situations	crossroads
tipping points	tests & ordeals	accidents	coincidences	secrets
growth/expansion	decline	forward progress	stagnation	strokes of luck
endings	ruts or habits	decisions	course corrections	looking for answers
retreat	risk & innovation	cultivation	watch & wait	adaptation
asking an expert	long-term plans	handing down/legacies	surrenders	

THE FOOL. | THE MAGICIAN. | THE HIGH PRIESTESS | THE EMPRESS. | THE EMPEROR. | THE HIEROPHANT

THE LOVERS. | THE CHARIOT. | STRENGTH. | THE HERMIT | WHEEL of FORTUNE | JUSTICE.

THE HANGED MAN. | DEATH. | TEMPERANCE | THE DEVIL. | THE TOWER. | THE STAR.

THE MOON | THE SUN. | JUDGEMENT. | THE WORLD.

Assignment 2.3

Four Suits Backward: Elements

Before we look at the minor arcana specifically, we're going to kind of take a bird's-eye view of the four suits. I generally believe in folks coming up with their own correspondences, but when it comes to the four suits, it's a good idea to play it a little more by the book. The four traditional elements—fire, water, air, earth—correspond to the four tarot suits by design. If you use any deck in the Golden Dawn tradition (that's Rider-Waite-Smith, Thoth, and all of their descendants in the English-speaking world), those four elements are going to structurally match the suits in the following way:

Fire = Wands

Water = Cups

Air = Swords

Earth = Pentacles or Disks

There are certainly traditions where you'll see something different (fire and air, in particular, have a tendency to swap places). But if you're going to get into correspondences with a conventional deck, you might as well start with these assumptions, since things will make a lot more sense later if you do.

Have a look at the qualities listed and decide how you'd like to assign them to the four suits. Some will be pretty straightforward. For example, chances are you're going to assign "feelings" to water, because practically everyone associates feelings with cups. But others may cause you to pause and take stock. Take the idea of "appetites." Some people are going to say that's associated with earth because it has to do with bodies and things you consume. But some people are going to say that's associated with fire, because it's a drive or hunger, a life force thing. There's some flex in interpretation, and that's all right.

Is there a traditional "right" answer for the four compass directions and for the humoral qualities (cool, wet, warm, dry, etc.)? Yes. You're welcome to look them up if you like. But it's also okay to simply assign them in whatever way seems most intuitive to you. If you don't assign "wet" to "water," I'm not sure where you're coming from, but hey! It takes all kinds.

Instructions

1 | In the center of your workspace, lay out the four elemental symbols as pictured. Or you can use physical objects representing them, like a candle, a cup of water, a feather, and a rock. Or you can just write the words in the middle of a piece of paper.

2 | Separate out the four suits from your deck and sort them into Wands, Cups, Swords, and Pentacles. (Don't worry about the major arcana for now.)

3 | Fan out the Wands in the fire quadrant, the Cups in the water quadrant, the Swords in the air quadrant, and the Pentacles in the earth quadrant.

4 | Assign the following terms and concepts, one to each quadrant.

cool & moist | cool & dry | warm & dry | warm & moist | north
east | south | west | goods & products | patterns | appetites
intimacy | drives | ambition | expectations | feelings | beliefs
money | desire | comforts | connection | inspiration | food
sex | words | routines | art | action | bodies | adventure
intellect | material resources | conflicts | leadership | intuition
arguments | creations | spirituality | empathy | caring

Assignment 2.4

Minor Arcana Backward: Moods

One easy way to capture the essence of each minor arcana card is to think of it as a mood. In many cases, you'll get an inkling of one mood the card may express just by examining the face of the figure on it. But even in the cases where there are no human figures (looking at you, 3 of Swords and 8 of Wands!), you can generally pick up a sense of emotional atmosphere.

Instructions

1 | Spread all forty minors out in front of you.

2 | Look at the following list and match up moods and minors. These are not exact one-to-one matches: sometimes more than one term will apply to the same card, and you should feel free to add your own! Assign at least one mood keyword to each minor card. Remember, there are *no wrong answers!* Just choose what makes sense for you.

calm | angry | curious | bored | excited | sympathetic

distressed | stubborn | caring | satisfied | defensive | friendly

anxious | determined | anticipating | happy | frustrated | resentful

argumentative | exasperated | respectful | mournful | pitying

self-pitying | pensive | compassionate | liberated | watchful

lonely | focused | frantic | overconfident | dreamy | nurturing

hurtful | complacent | worn out | cautious | overwhelmed

incredulous | fascinated | proud | smug | breathless | combative

wary | distracted | uncertain | doubtful | sad | embarrassed

pleased | gloating | desperate | patient | contented

_____   _____   _____   _____   _____

_____   _____   _____   _____   _____

_____   _____   _____   _____   _____

_____   _____   _____   _____   _____

Assignment 2.5

Minor Arcana Backward: Everyday Occurrences

In this assignment, you'll consider forty everyday scenarios you might recognize from your own life. Just to make things slightly easier, I've split them up by suits. For each suit you'll consider ten different—but very ordinary—life experiences, and you'll assign them to a card from the appropriate suit. You might not agree with every one of the life experiences that I've described. That's totally okay! Feel free to come up with your own scenarios, as long as you come up with at least one for each card.

Wands

- Sent off my grant application. Fingers crossed.

- Moved my mom into assisted living.

- Bright idea for a new game!

- Looked at new houses.

- That article about my project came out!

- Argument about "whose job it is" to do the dumb chore.

- Lots of Amazon deliveries in the mail.

- Went to a weekend wedding.

- Pushed myself really hard in my workout.

- Got it all done even with a headache. That's how tough I am.

ACE of WANDS.

_____

_____

_____

Cups

- Delightful birthday outing to the theatre.
- Went to my niece's baptism.
- Walked away from an argument.
- Netflix and chill.
- Watched a dramatic sunset after the rain.
- Went to my grandfather's funeral.
- Girls' night out!
- Planted a flower garden with my kids.
- Attended a graduation party.
- Bought two quarts of milk.

ACE OF CUPS.

_____

_____

_____

II

_____

_____

_____

III

_____

_____

_____

IV

_____

_____

_____

V

_____

_____

_____

VI

_____

_____

_____

VII

_____

_____

_____

VIII

_____

_____

_____

IX

_____

_____

_____

X

_____

_____

_____

Swords

- Mediated a dispute between my brother and my aunt.

- Started looking at job listings so I can get out of this dump.

- Got a splinter while thinking about my ex.

- Had a long morning meditation.

- Who will know if I help myself to some sticky notes from the supply closet?

- Really tired and discouraged; just wanted to go back to bed.

- Heard Lauren from high school made CEO last week. Ugh.

- Finally cut down that weed tree in the backyard.

- Frustrated with tech problems at work.

- Woke up in a cold sweat. Thought I overslept on the big day.

_____

_____

_____

_____

_____

_____

_____

_____

_____

_____

_____

_____

_____

_____

_____

_____

_____

_____

_____

_____

_____

_____

_____

_____

_____

_____

_____

_____

_____

_____

Pentacles

- Family reunion! Totally overate.

- Made a deposit in my IRA.

- Got a small bonus and invested it in on home improvement.

- Decorated my single-and-loving-it apartment.

- Spent all day planting bulbs. Hope they come up next spring.

- Opportunity for a promotion!

- Tripped outside church and sprained my ankle.

- Successfully collaborated on something with my colleagues.

- Got involved in a project and stayed late at work.

- Multitasked like a champ.

Assignment 2.6

Court Cards Backward: People and Professions

The sixteen court cards of a tarot deck are notoriously difficult to interpret. So for this exercise, we're going to start with some rank and suit keywords to supplement what you see on the card. Feel free to substitute your own keywords, including the ones you just came up with in Assignment 2.3: Four Suits Backward.

For example: let's consider the formidable Queen of Swords. If I use the keywords *connecting* for Queen and *thoughts/words/conflicts* for Swords, I know the Queen of Swords must be a *connector of thoughts or words*. When I look at the list of professions, I see "editor" on the list, and I know that an editor connects thoughts and words, so I know that's one role this court card can play.

Instructions

1 | Start by using keywords to describe each court card; e.g., *connector* of *thoughts* for Queen of Swords. You can use the keywords I've suggested, or come up with your own.

> **Page:** Reflecting or studying; messengers
>
> **Knight:** Acting or reacting; agents
>
> **Queen:** Connecting; pattern experts
>
> **King:** Guiding/directing; strategists
>
> **Wands:** Drives/ambitions/appetites; fire
>
> **Cups:** Emotions/art/spirituality; water
>
> **Swords:** Thoughts/words/conflicts; air
>
> **Pentacles:** Things/bodies/money/food; earth

2 | Look at the following list of people and professions. Match them to a court card, using keywords, symbols on the cards, facial expressions, body language, or whatever works for you. Remember, this is fuzzy logic: sometimes more than one term will apply to the same card, and you should feel free to add your own. Assign at least one profession keyword to each court card. Remember, there are *no wrong answers!*

3 | Come up with more professions if you like.

student | librarian | entrepreneur | fortune teller | socialite | waiter
gardener | artist | teacher/professor | spiritual leader | military general
inventor | cook/chef | accountant | bouncer | athlete
massage therapist | administrator | journalist | doctor
bed-and-breakfast owner | stock clerk | dairy farmer | construction worker
veterinarian | bodyguard | actor | truck driver | software engineer
courier | salesperson | web designer | stunt person | fundraiser
film producer | sportscaster | mechanical engineer | psychotherapist
rock star | pilot | editor | choreographer | seamstress | plumber
car designer | spy | police officer | diplomat | conscientious objector

_____   _____   _____   _____

_____   _____   _____   _____

_____   _____   _____   _____

_____   _____   _____   _____

Assignment 2.7

Court Cards Backward: Labels

In real life, I think labels are terribly unhelpful. After all, each one of us is nuanced, complex, three-dimensional—I contain multitudes! And so do you! These are unabashed caricatures, shadow selves that we project onto other human beings (and, in weak moments, on ourselves).

I hope you don't think of yourself, in your heart of hearts, as a poser or a narcissist or a control freak. But that said, these cartoon characterizations are so extreme they can help us understand some of the reflections cast by the court cards, roles that they—and we—may play from time to time. Plus, it's just kind of fun.

Instructions

1 | Refer back to your list of court keywords from the previous exercise.

2 | Look at the following list of labels. Match them to a court card, using keywords, symbols on the cards, facial expressions, body language, or whatever works for you. Remember, this is fuzzy logic: sometimes more than one term will apply to the same card, and you should feel free to add your own. Assign at least one label to each court card. Remember, there are *no wrong answers!*

3 | Add more labels if you wish.

user | seducer | ditz | people pleaser | poser | artiste
con artist | elder statesperson | peacemaker | live wire | social butterfly
loner | queen bee | flirt | manipulator | helicopter parent
narcissist | overachiever | slacker | joe schmo | nerd | jock
squeaky wheel | hipster | sophisticate | control freak | loose cannon
enabler | thug | snowflake | hipster | fashionista

_____   _____   _____   _____

_____   _____   _____   _____

_____   _____   _____   _____

_____   _____   _____   _____

Chapter 2 Final Assignment

Portrait of a Day

Congratulations! You've made it to the end of Backward Tarot. It's time to take your rapidly developing tarot language for a spin. In the last chapter, you looked for matches to a card chosen for you by Fate! In this chapter, because we're working backward, you will be the one deliberately choosing cards to describe your day.

Instructions

1 | Choose one day that you will closely observe in all its aspects. Pay attention to circumstances beyond your control and how you reacted to them (which might remind you of the "trends" or "building blocks of personhood" you observed in your major arcana assignments), feelings you experienced and things that happened (which might remind you of the "moods" and "everyday occurrences" you thought about in your minor arcana assignments), and the people you encountered and the roles they fulfilled (which might remind you of the "professions" and "labels" you mulled over in your court cards assignments).

2 | Make a list of the following:

- Circumstances beyond your control or not of your making

  – Describe using majors

- Themes you thought about

  – Describe using majors

- Moods you experienced

  – Describe using minors

- Things that happened, which may also include things you read or heard, or things that happened to others around you

  – Describe using minors

- People you encountered

  – Describe using courts

3 | Try and figure out what tarot card represents each of these different components of your day. Choose a card to describe each, and—if it's not obvious—make a note of

why you chose that one. Try to come up with at least ten cards to form the portrait of your day.

Need some examples?

- **Circumstances Beyond My Control:** It was a really beautiful, hot day today. The AC in my car wasn't working, so I opened my windows.

  – The Sun

- **Themes I Thought About:** I looked at my old yearbook pictures and thought about how much all of our lives have changed since graduation. I barely recognize myself!

  – Death

- **Moods I Experienced:** I snuck kale into my son's meatloaf and he loved it! I felt sneaky but resourceful.

  – 7 of Swords

- **Things That Happened:** I went for a walk in the dog park. Everyone seemed to be in a really good mood. I literally saw a rainbow!

  – 10 of Cups

- **People I Encountered:** I met up with my uncle, who talked about the wine-tasting course he just took and how much he enjoyed it.

  – King of Pentacles

4 | Your turn!

- **Circumstances Beyond My Control:**

  _____

  _____

  _____

  – Card: _____

- **Themes I Thought About:**

  _____

  _____

  _____

  – Card: _____

• Moods I Experienced:

_____

_____

_____

   – Card: _____

• Things That Happened:

_____

_____

_____

   – Card: _____

• People I Encountered:

_____

_____

_____

   – Card: _____

Three
TAROT FORWARD

You, too, can map reality.

Tarot Backward worked with things you know already. Tarot Forward helps you develop keywords, systems, chains of association—a kind of structural scaffolding to help you explore each card's subsurface dimensions. For example, I might look at the 4 of Pentacles and see only the idea of miserliness or stinginess. But if I put together the concept I associate with 4s ("gathering") with the concept I associate with Pentacles ("material resources"), I have a map I can use to go in many different directions. *"Gathering* of *material resources"* could indeed be miserliness. But it could also be a bank, or a company, or even a family, since families typically pool (or "gather") their earnings (or "material resources").

Now, you may rightly observe that these kinds of keywords show up in every Little White Book that comes with a tarot deck. Why should you come up with more? Here's the answer: the process of growing those keywords from scratch, systematically, means that they stick a lot better than they do if you just straight-up memorize someone else's vague notion of what a given card is about.

Tarot is a sky full of stars! And it is your job to name the constellations as if you were the first human being to ever see them. As that beautiful web of associations grows in your mind, you will be able to describe anything in life using a tarot card.

Tarot Forward, then, is about building systems of correspondences. *But wait!* you might interject, astutely. *Aren't there already systems of correspondences for tarot?* You're right! There are!

The Hermetic Order of the Golden Dawn (from which, in 1910, the Rider-Waite-Smith tarot deck arose, like Aphrodite emerging from the sea) assigned all manner of correspondences to the cards. I wrote a whole book on them, and I use them all the time.[6] If you're into astrology or Hermetic Kabbalah or Renaissance magic, you may like using them too.

But the point of this section is that you *don't have to*. The Golden Dawn correspondences are simply a system someone came up with, and you're someone too. You are a human being with an active consciousness and a healthy imagination, which means you have as good an idea of what the number four means as anybody. And you're going to use those innate resources of yours to develop your own correspondences—that is to say, your own X-ray vision that lets you see *through* the surface of the card and into the "cloud of cognition" that surrounds it.

All Roads Lead to Rome

Sometimes it'll be easy to figure out what card goes with what thing in your life. Sometimes it might not be so easy. For example, in the previous chapter I mentioned tying shoelaces. Personally, I associate the 2 of Pentacles with tying my shoes. Why? Lots of reasons.

- There's an infinity sign on it that looks like shoelaces.
- Its Hermetic title is the "Lord of Change." I tie my shoelaces when I'm about to transition from one part of my day to the next.
- It's associated with the planet Jupiter in the sign of Capricorn, which is ruled by Saturn. Jupiter and Saturn represent concepts of freedom and limitation, respectively. When I tie my shoes, I'm limiting the way they can relate to my body. I'm binding them (Saturn) to my feet, which gives me the freedom (Jupiter) to do all kinds of things.

As you can see, I use correspondences to help me get there: zodiacal correspondences, planetary correspondences, the symbolic correspondence of the infinity sign, and the Hermetic title. *But you don't have to.* For example, maybe you associate the 7 of Wands with tying your shoes. This could be because:

- You had a coach who always wore green and was constantly telling you to tie your shoes before practice.

---

6 | T. Susan Chang, *Tarot Correspondences: Ancient Secrets for Everyday Readers* (Woodbury, MN: Llewellyn Publications, 2018).

- It's a 7, and tying your shoes is something you do at 7:00 a.m. every morning.
- If you look at the right shoe of the figure in the 7 of Wands, *you can actually see an untied shoelace.*

My point is that it doesn't matter *how* you come up with which card reminds you of tying your shoes, or checking out your groceries, or planting your fall bulbs. It doesn't even matter if it's not always the same card. There are synonyms—different ways of saying the same thing—throughout the deck, just as there are in language itself. What matters is that, if you try, you can come up with a card to describe each of those things in a personally meaningful way.

With each Tarot Forward exercise, you'll be encouraging your mind to stretch out tendrils in every direction, extending and complexifying the gorgeous neurome which, in the end, is what makes you *you*.

At some point, you will find you have a "tarot brain" living right inside your normal brain. You'll walk past an arbor decorated with cut flowers and a little voice inside you will shout, "4 of Wands!" And if you're lucky, someone will kiss you there, in a very 4 of Wands way, and, my friend, you will be *living the poem*.

Chapter 3 Assignments: An Overview

In last chapter's Tarot Backward assignments, I gave you lists of ideas and you matched them up with the major arcana, the minor arcana, and the court cards. In this chapter's assignments, you'll be coming up with the ideas and concepts yourself.

When you first got your deck, maybe your first evening with the cards went something like this: You sat there staring at the Chariot and thinking, *Momentum? Battle? Determination?* But the wheels on the Chariot don't look like they turn, and the guy seems to be waist-deep in a concrete block, and his expression looks weirdly passive. *Stoicism? Stasis?* And those sphinxes! What the hell! *Mysteries? Cryptozoology?!* You're only seven words into this thing and you're already confused.

You know what these chapter 3 assignments are *not* like? That.

Think of these assignments as a game, like Pictionary or Apples to Apples or Cards Against Humanity or Ransom Notes. There's a prompt, but then you have a specific set of tools and a framework in which your creative imagination gets to run wild. Figuratively speaking, you have game pieces, or Monopoly money, or poker chips, or Scrabble tiles.

For some of us, what makes a game a game is an audience. So do these with a friend, if you like. If you need stakes—i.e., you need to feel like you won or lost—do them with a group and take turns being the judge. Who came up with the wackiest title for the Hermit? What about the Queen of Wands? *Who came up with* shitposting *for the 8 of Wands?* Mansplaining *for the 9 of Cups?* Have prizes if you want. Do them slightly buzzed if you want. I'm not here to judge your life!

And if you just want to hole up by yourself in your book-lined bedroom to do these, with the cat and a pot of tea and maybe some knitting for when you need a change of pace, that's cool too.

* * * * * *

Assignment 3.1
Major Arcana Forward: Make Up Your Own Titles

Our first Tarot Forward assignment is pure entertainment. I hope it will convince you that growing the skeletal structure that is Tarot Forward is not a chore so much as an act of mercurial play—one that can be as goofy as you want it to be.

As you may or may not know, the Golden Dawn came up with a set of elevated, rather pretentious-sounding titles describing every card in the deck. For example, the Lovers are called "the Children of the Voice Divine" and "the Oracles of the Mighty Gods." The Death card is called "the Child of the Great Transformers, the Lord of the Gates of Death." The Tower is "the Lord of the Hosts of the Mighty." There's a lot of "mighty" in here, and a lot of "Lords."

But we don't have to use those titles. We can make up our own! I've created a list of "honorific" titles you can start out with: Lord, Lady, Father, Mother, Guardian, Angel, Keeper, etc. Pick one of those (or come up with your own) and then look at the major arcana and hunt for a symbol you find appealing.

Let's take the Hermit. For a fairly minimalist card, it's quite rich with concrete symbols: lantern, staff, mountain, robes, snow. You could call him "the Bringer of the Lantern." You could call him "the Holder of the Staff." Or the Sun card—it's got sunflowers on it. You could call it "the Spirit of the Sunflowers" or "the Rider of the White Horse" (although I guess Death could also be "the Rider of the White Horse"). One of my students named Death "the Suit Stripper" and the Wheel of Fortune "the Holy Escalator." Another named the Fool "the Captain of Falling with Style." These made me spit my tea. You too can make someone spit their tea.

Have fun! I think you'll find the process helps you solidify some of these archetypal images in your mind.

Instructions

1 | Lay out all twenty-two major arcana. Choose any one to start with.

2 | Pick an "honorific" from the list provided, or make up one of your own.

3 | Choose any symbol you see in the card and combine it with the honorific to come up with your own Hermetic title for the card!

daughter | son | child | guardian | father | mother | prince
knight | queen | king | princess | lord | lady | ruler
keeper | holder | explorer | angel | demon | servant
teacher | creature | bringer | bane | god/dess | divinity
mistress | master | spirit | great one | leader | warrior
guide | warden | architect | source | sovereign

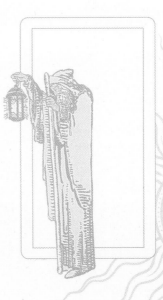

THE FOOL.

THE MAGICIAN.

THE HIGH PRIESTESS

THE EMPRESS.

THE EMPEROR.

THE HIEROPHANT

THE LOVERS.

THE CHARIOT.

STRENGTH.

THE HERMIT.

WHEEL of FORTUNE

JUSTICE.

THE HANGED MAN.

DEATH.

TEMPERANCE.

THE DEVIL.

THE TOWER.

THE STAR.

THE MOON.

THE SUN.

JUDGEMENT.

THE WORLD.

Assignment 3.2

Minor Arcana Forward:
Make Up Your Own Number Correspondences

For this exercise, you're going to take out only the numbered minor arcana in your deck: Ace through 10 in each of the four suits. You're going to organize them by number, looking at just four cards at a time: all four Aces, all four 2s, etc.

As you look at each set of four cards, you're going to try and figure out what they have in common—because they really do have something in common, even if it's not obvious at first glance. See if you can come up with a few different keywords that might work for each set of four. Then, sleep on it for a day or two. (This is important. Those keywords need to wriggle their way down into your subconscious. And Tomorrow Brain is always better than Today Brain when it comes to refining ideas.)

Finally, see if you can narrow it down to one keyword that you really, really like. You're not married to that keyword—you might tweak it a year from now, or two or ten. But it's good to have something to start with.

This is going to be very useful when you're in the middle of a reading and you come across the 7 of Pentacles and suddenly have no idea what it means. You pause and ask yourself, *What was my keyword for sevens? How is this card like a seven?* and that will help get the train going again.

Instructions

1 | Sort out all your numbered minor arcana, Ace through 10 in each suit.

2 | Group them by number—all the Aces, all the 2s, etc.

3 | Come up with keywords, a few for each group of numbered minors. Give yourself some time to think it over, then narrow it down to one keyword per set of numbers. (Example: for the 8s, *organizing* or *production*.)

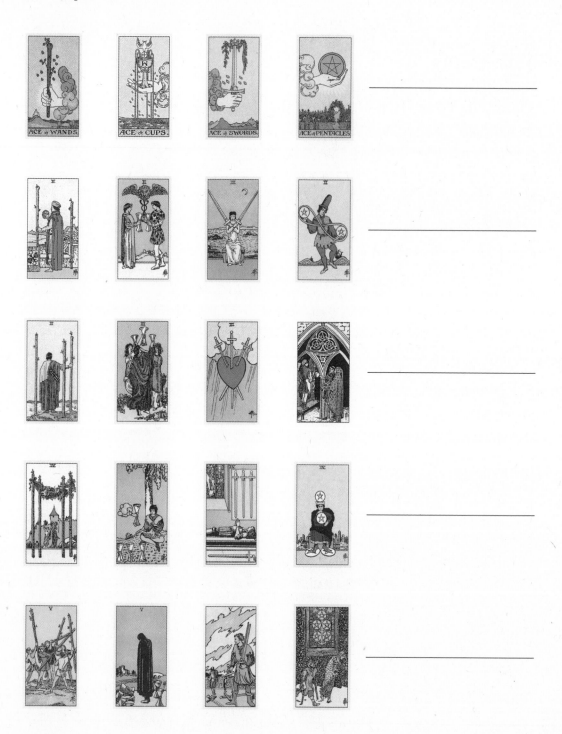

Assignment 3.3

Minor Arcana Forward:
Make Up Your Own Individual Keywords

You might know that the Golden Dawn gave each of the minor arcana cards a "Hermetic title": for example, the 3 of Wands is the "Lord of Virtue." The 8 of Cups is the "Lord of Indolence." Some of these have survived the last century better than others.

Those titles and keywords were just somebody's bright idea, and you can have a bright idea too. There's something to be said for coming up with your own keywords, and that's what this exercise is about.

Here's how it works. You're going to look at the card in question. Let's suppose it's our old friend, the 4 of Pentacles. *What number is it?* 4, obviously. You're going to go back to your number keyword sheet (Assignment 3.2) and find that perfect keyword you came up with for 4s. *What suit is it?* Pentacles, obviously. You're going to go back to your four elements/ four suits exercise (Assignment 2.3) from chapter 2 and choose a keyword from that to represent the suit in question. Try a bunch until you find the one that seems to work best.

So, for example—as I've mentioned before—the keyword I use for 4s is "gathering." And generally, when I think of a keyword for Pentacles, I start with "material resources." When I look at the 4 of Pentacles, I think to myself, *That's a* gathering *of* material resources. If I start with that phrase, "gathering of material resources," how can I distill it down to a single word? I could do it a number of ways. It could be "hoarding." It could be "storage" or "treasure" or "accumulation." For this exercise, you're going to settle on the one word that you think best describes that idea. And then you're going to do that for the other thirty-nine cards, because we are tarot nerds and that is how we roll.

Instructions

1 | Fill in the number keywords you came up with in Assignment 3.2 in the following table.

2 | Fill in the suit keywords you came up with in Assignment 2.3 in the following table.

3 | Combine them (i.e. a *gathering* of *material resources*) and try to come up with a single word that sums up that idea.

Number	Keyword
1	
2	
3	
4	
5	
6	
7	
8	
9	
10	

Suit	Keyword
Wands	
Cups	
Swords	
Pentacles	

_____   _____   _____   _____   _____

_____   _____   _____   _____   _____

_____   _____   _____   _____   _____

_____   _____   _____   _____   _____

_____   _____   _____   _____   _____

_____   _____   _____   _____   _____

_____   _____   _____   _____   _____

_____   _____   _____   _____   _____

Assignment 3.4

Court Cards Forward: Elemental Combinations

You might or might not know that the sixteen court cards traditionally have elemental correspondences. For example, the Queen of Swords is—cryptically—known as the *watery part of air*. As usual, this is the doing of the Golden Dawn. We use Golden Dawn correspondences sparingly in this book, but as with Assignment 2.3, this is one of those times.

Ranks have elemental correspondences, like so:

King = Fire

Queen = Water

Knight = Air

Page = Earth

And, as we know, suits have elemental correspondences, like so:

Wands = Fire

Cups = Water

Swords = Air

Pentacles = Earth

Put these together and you can come up with a table like this:

	△ Fire	▽ Water	⟁ Air	▽ Earth
Fire △	King of Wands	King of Cups	King of Swords	King of Pentacles
Water ▽	Queen of Wands	Queen of Cups	Queen of Swords	Queen of Pentacles
Air ⟁	Knight of Wands	Knight of Cups	Knight of Swords	Knight of Pentacles
Earth ▽	Page of Wands	Page of Cups	Page of Swords	Page of Pentacles

When the Golden Dawn refers to "parts" of elements—i.e., the "watery part of air"—I believe they're speaking about mostly nonphysical qualities. To say that "air" has a "watery part" is to say that air can have a fluid, connecting sort of quality within its weightless, mobile nature. And that is something we can also say of the Queen of Swords.

For this exercise, we're going to imagine, in a literal way, how the four elements combine in the physical world. When you see a lot of earth, things may be very stable and grounded—or they may be stuck or stagnant. When you combine two elements, more complex phenomena arise. What happens when you add air to fire? (A lot of air, a little fire: the fire goes out! A little air, a lot of fire: the fire grows!) Water to earth? (Mud! Good for growing things!) It's always worth looking at the balance of elements in your readings.

So, to consider our example of the Queen of Swords, let's think about how air and water combine. You could have bubbles. You could have mist and fog. You could have clouds. By thinking about how elements combine, you can get insight into the character of the courts. Just remember, when you're combining the two elements in a court card, the *suit* is the dominant element. The Queen of Swords (Water of *Air*) might be more like a cloud; the Knight of Cups (Air of *Water*) might be more like a fountain.

Instructions

With that in mind, here is a table to start filling out.

1 | Look at the elemental combination corresponding to each of these boxes (i.e., Queen of Wands = water and fire). Come up with a natural phenomenon that combines those two elements. In fact, feel free to come up with several! For the "pure" combinations ("fire of fire," "water of water," "air of air," and "earth of earth"), try and think of phenomena that truly seem to symbolize the most unadulterated expression of that element. For example, for "earth of earth," you might have something that is crystallized within the earth—a literal crystal or fossil, say.

2 | Once you've done that, come up with some nicknames for your courts—the more absurd the better. For example, you could call the Queen of Wands "the Queen of the Hot Springs," if you wanted, and you could imagine Old Faithful erupting behind her throne on the card. Because, as the German Resistance used to sing in the bad old days of World War II, *Die Gedanken sind frei!* In other words: *thinking is free,* and ain't nobody gonna stop you.

	Fire / Wands	Water / Cups	Air / Swords	Earth / Pentacles
Fire / King				
Water / Queen				
Air / Knight				
Earth / Page				

A few keywords just to start you off:

mist | lava | marshes | stars | hair dryers | fossils

caves | tornadoes | hot springs | radiant floors | currents

breezes | riverbanks | coals | blizzards | lakes

lightning | volcanoes | bubbles | cyclones

Assignment 3.5

What's Your Jam? Create Your Own Correspondences

What do you know more about than anybody else? What does your inner nerd delight in? Pro wrestling? Runes? Norse gods? Orisha? Myers-Briggs? Fixed stars? I Ching? Famous Hollywood celebrities? Spices? Nineties hip-hop? Mythological animals? Vintage video games? Craft brews? Noble truths of Buddhism? Marvel superheroes? Imported cars? Doritos flavors?

Anything you know by heart can be the basis of a set of correspondences. Twenty-two amino acids? Assign them to the majors! Gryffindor, Slytherin, Ravenclaw, Hufflepuff? Assign them to the suits! (Are Slytherins Cups, or not? Tarot readers love to debate this.) You can use real things, or you can use abstract concepts, or you can use fictional worlds; it doesn't matter.

Whatever it is, that's what you're going to use to make up your own tarot correspondences in this exercise. Your subject matter just has to be something that comes in several different varieties and that you know at a pretty granular level.

Choose your set of:

• Four (suits)

• Ten (Ace to 10)

• Sixteen (court cards)

• Twenty-two (majors)

• Thirty-six (2–10 minors)

• Or even…all seventy-eight cards in the deck

You don't have to have exactly four or ten or twenty-two of anything to start. For example, there are said to be 401 Orisha divinities, but you could just choose the four or ten or sixteen that are the most meaningful to you. The point of the exercise is to draw connections that fill in a complete map of your personal reality.

Over the years, I've come to look forward to the moment when my students get to this assignment. It's always a window into a wacky and wonderful private world. Sometimes it's a passion they've felt reluctant to share with the outer world. Most seem to choose the set of twenty-two (majors). I've seen the majors as Bob Dylan songs, yoga poses, herbs and spices, JFK conspiracy theory elements, favorite poems, and figures out of Greek myth. I've seen the court cards corresponding to sixteen phonemes in the English language. I've seen a list of seventy-eight horror movies corresponding one-to-one to the cards, and even a list of seventy-eight fonts!

My point is, *have fun with it!* Tarot can accommodate everything in life, and it absolutely, positively can accommodate that thing you love the most.

_____

_____

_____

_____

_____

_____

_____

_____

_____

_____

_____

_____

_____

_____

Chapter 3 Final Assignment

DIY Correspondence Chart

Create a correspondence chart of the majors or the minors (or both, if you're ambitious), using your favorite system of correspondences. You've done all of the assignments in chapters 2 and 3, and you've made all kinds of connections between tarot and the outer world, or tarot and not-tarot.

- You've learned that the suit of Cups is watery.
- You've given the majors nicknames (The Holy Escalator! The Spirit of the Unsaid Remark! The Servant of the Tree House!).[7]
- You've connected that day you and your kids planted a flower garden with the 6 of Cups.
- You've hypothesized that the Knight of Swords might be a police officer, or maybe a "loose cannon," or possibly even a cyclone.

In other words, you've developed a private language, a kind of infrastructure for your tarot vision as it grows deeper and more acute. This final assignment is a way of driving those associations deeper into your memory and helping them stick.

You're going to do that by creating something beautiful. And when I say that, I don't mean that you have to be an artist. The fact is, organized information is inherently beautiful. You can do this assignment with a ruler or compass or graph paper, or you can do it freehand. It can be in circular form, table form, or it can be a diagram. One ingenious student of mine, determined to work with a perfect circle, actually painted hers on a vinyl record!

The only thing I ask is that you don't just download a table into a spreadsheet or something, since that sort of misses the point. By making something with your hands, you force yourself to experience every word that you write—every glyph, every dot, every colored line—in real time. Dedicating yourself to that effort sears it into your brain, and you won't get the benefit of that if you just print something out.

I've found that many folks like using the Golden Dawn correspondences—especially the astrological ones—to do this assignment, and if you want to do that, you'll probably find *Tarot Correspondences* to be a useful guide. But you don't have to use Golden Dawn correspondences.

---

7 | That's the Wheel of Fortune (from Alan Scalpone), the Hermit (from Dana Welts), and the Hanged Man (from Nya Thryce). Thanks as always to my students for their ingenious contributions!

You could remap the Tree of Life; you could work with runes or geomantic figures; you could use any of the concepts you've joined up with the cards so far. Any correspondence system your brain has a hunger to master is fair game.

Instructions

1 | Choose a set of correspondences: your own, or one based on an esoteric system. The set should include all twenty-two major arcana, all fifty-six minor arcana, *OR* all seventy-eight cards.

2 | Visually express the correspondences as a chart or diagram. It can be round or square or Tree of Life–shaped—whatever is most pleasing to your eye. Give it color; include any meaningful symbols, sigils, ideograms, or pictures you wish. You want something so visually appealing that you'd be happy to have it hanging it on your wall!

3 | Hang it on your wall. (*Optional.*)

————

Congratulations! You've completed chapters 2 and 3, which are the research and study portion of the workbook. In the coming chapters, we're going to move on to applying the network of ideas you put together here.

But I hope you return to these thought experiments now and again—I know I do. There's never a moment when we stop learning, or when we stop making connections with our tarot brain. I still find myself pausing and asking, when I'm at the car wash or the dentist's waiting room, or when I've just eaten more cookies than I meant to: *What would this look like in tarot?* It never ends. And that's a feature, not a bug.

interlude
UPSIDE DOWN AND INSIDE OUT—ALL ABOUT REVERSALS

Okay. Take a deep breath! In chapter 2 and chapter 3 we applied some serious mental torque to the cards to come up with interpretations that stick and feel meaningful. Now—before we move on to applying that freshly hewn infrastructure to a reading—I'd like to take a moment to address an issue every reader has to reckon with at some point: reversals.

Pick ten tarot readers and you'll get ten different opinions about reversals, those cards that come out of the deck upside down. What follows is my attempt to summarize my own viewpoint on reversals. Hopefully, these observations will help you come to your own conclusions about whether using reversals is right for you.

Use Them? Don't Use Them? Sort of Use Them?

Three schools of thought on reversals exist.

1 | **Don't use them.** Tarot readers who don't use reversals simply turn the card around if it comes out upside down; they pretend it didn't happen. This is perfectly legitimate.

2 | **Sort of use them.** Some readers take care to always shuffle so the cards come out upright, but once in a while there's a card that comes out reversed, or there's a "jumper," a card that falls out of the deck reversed or upright. Some readers think jumpers and accidental reversals have special meaning: it's a card to pay attention to, or a card that

should have been in the spread, or one with a special message for the querent. This is also valid.

3 | **Do use them.** And then there are some readers who use reversals all the time. I'm one of them. As I've said before, even just one-seventy-eighth of *everything in the world* is still a pretty huge chunk of life. Reversals help guide me toward the right section of the interpretational sphere; they add nuance and dimension and gray areas. And I love gray areas.

I love reversals, and I've read with them more or less since I started reading tarot twenty-five years ago. Now, those of us who like reversals are in the minority, but I'm going to make a case why you might want to use them and you can decide for yourself.

How and Why Do You Do It?

If you want to use reversals, it's easy to start. Just divide the deck in half and turn one half upside down before you shuffle. Shuffle a few times, and voilà! half your cards are upside down and randomly distributed through the deck. Now that you're ready to read reversals, here's a few things to keep in mind.

Reversals don't have to be negative. Many people read as if a reversed card is simply a card gone bad—the opposite of its cheery upright self. I firmly disagree with this. I think if you want to say something negative in tarot, there are plenty of ways to say it without needing to consider reversals negative. It's also a statistical problem. Many people read the deck, upright, as mostly positive. So when they introduce reversals, suddenly they see a world where half the things that are happening are entirely negative. The Queen of Swords reversed is a bitch-queen; the 10 of Cups reversed is a loss of all your happiness; the Magician reversed is a charlatan. Most of us are lucky enough not to view our lives as 50 percent evil and dark, and we work, consciously or unconsciously, to keep it that way. Thinking in black and white is not that helpful to us as readers. I prefer to think that every card is a spectrum with light and dark ends—and the card itself is neutral.

The practice of reading reversals as negative does have strong roots in tradition. For example, in eighteenth-century cartomancy, it was not unusual for people to read reversed cards as representing essentially the opposite of the upright meaning of the card. Sometimes that meant that the reversed card took on a distinctly negative connotation. For example, in *Manière de tirer le grand Etteilla où tarots Egyptiens*, Etteilla characterizes the 2 of Cups as *amour heureux* ("happy love"). But reversed, he proclaims, it signifies *désir d'amour qui ne sera pas satisfait* ("desire for love which will not be satisfied").[8] This "reversals as opposite" tradition would also influence the Rider-Waite-Smith tarot.

8 | Etteilla, *Maniere de tirer le grand Etteilla ou tarots Égyptiens* (Paris: P. B. Grimaud, 1954).

If you read *The Pictorial Key to the Tarot,* Arthur Edward Waite's book on the Rider-Waite-Smith tarot, you will see that he often used reversed meanings to turn the upright meaning of the card into its opposite. For example, Waite associates the 6 of Cups with the past, just as many modern readers do today—but then, he says, the 6 of Cups reversed must have to do with the future! Similarly, Waite views the upright Ace of Wands as "creation, invention"; the reversed Ace is "fall, decadence."[9] I find this counterintuitive and overly simplistic. If you consider the 5 of Cups to indicate grief and loss, does its reversal now signify joy and celebration? I just don't see it. I can see grief and loss subsiding, perhaps, but that doesn't mean it's a party.

I think that the energy of the card is the energy of the card. It may be changed in some way; it may be distorted in some way; it may be on its way in or out. But I believe that these are matters of perspective that come with the reader, not with the card.

I think of reversals as creating motion in a stable structure—sort of like shuffling, or when you cast a handful of grains in the air. My understanding of divination has to do with sensing a pattern in motion, the turning of the Wheel of Fortune, as opposed to a set arrangement of cause and effect that's fixed in stone. In other forms of divination, this motion is taken for granted. For example, when you consult the I Ching (or "The Book of *Changes*"), it is possible for your oracular hexagram to include one or more "moving lines," indicating that things are shifting. I think reversals fulfill a similar function in tarot.

In other words, reversals can represent an opportunity for things to turn out differently than how you thought they would. And that might be why I like them so much.

Reversals Can Energize a Visual Reading

Before I get into the main interpretive ways you can consider using reversals, I'm going to mention a couple of considerations from a visual perspective. For example, reversals can visually energize a reading by altering the line of the gaze. Consider court cards, which in a Rider-Waite-Smith or RWS-derived deck always feature people. Reversal allows a court card that normally looks left to look right, and vice versa, so it's looking at something other than what it would normally look at—or *someone* other than whom it would normally look at. You can do this with other side-facing cards as well, like the Hermit or the 2 of Wands.

Normally, the Page of Wands looks to the right. Reversed, it's looking to the left. So you can ask yourself, *What is the Page of Wands looking at now?* Maybe she's looking at someone else or something else in the reading. It's worth following that gaze wherever it goes. In fact, if the court card is all the way to one side of the reading and looking away from the other cards, you could even draw a card to see just what they're looking at. And that should give you some idea of what's in the mind of the figure on the card.

---

9 | Arthur Edward Waite, *The Pictorial Key to the Tarot* (Stamford, CT: US Games Systems, 1986), 196.

Another visual phenomenon that's worth considering with reversals is that they cause the lines of the cards to match up in different ways. Topography matters in tarot: a hill can turn into a horizon on the card next to it; a waterfall may join up with a pool (place the Empress next to the Star and see if you can spot the water flowing between them). When you read with reversals, the edge iconography of one card may now line up—or *not* line up—with its neighbor. Those of you who read with Tarot de Marseille decks will be very familiar with this technique of following the landscape through the cards, as if they were a sequence in a graphic novel.

It's even worth considering visual *gravity* when you're dealing with reversals. For example, if you turn over the Ace of Cups, all of a sudden everything's falling out. It's not being constantly replenished, like a fountain, the way it is when it's upright. The swords on the 10 of Swords may now be falling out of the figure's back and onto the head of the figure in the card below. That could be meaningful in the context of your reading.

Reversals can also add a sense of time to your readings. Very often, a figure who was looking right, into the future, will now be looking left, into the past—or vice versa.

Reversals Can Mean "It's Up to You"

One thing all reversal interpretations share is that there's a feeling that you're preoccupied with the card in some way; you're trying to work with its energy. When you draw the card upright, we might say it's kind of handed to you—it simply appears in your life whether because of external circumstances or actions you couldn't help taking. When the card comes out reversed, you can think of it as potential: sure, it could be a 3 of Cups day, but it will take a little conscious help from you to get there.

If this way of reading becomes part of your practice, it can be extremely powerful when you're using a larger spread. If you're looking at eight or ten cards and you see a lot of reversals, you can read that as meaning it's kind of up to your client what happens next. Suppose seven cards out of ten come out reversed: that might tell you that lots of things are in flux; that nothing is settled; that much is up to the querent's own actions and choices. The possibility of those cards is all there, but it's not happening without help. I believe that a ton of upright major arcana indicates that circumstances are, to some degree, out of your hands—you're dealing with large patterns in the web of fate. Following this line of reasoning, reversed cards—particularly minor reversed cards—could mean that your fate is very much in your hands. Reversals could reflect a certain level of uncertainty on your own part, or a moment when the linear narrative in the book of destiny suddenly forks and asks you to choose your own adventure. Maybe free will just plays a larger role when cards are upside down.

Reversals Can Mean "It's Not Straightforward"

Mostly I read reversals this way: the energy of the card is present, but it's not quite there in full force for whatever reason.

I like to think of a reversed card as being like the upright card, but qualified: as if the card has an asterisk, or its own little footnote. Something is not quite straightforward about it, and it's up to us to figure out, in the context of the reading, what that might be.

Suppose you get the 3 of Cups, a card of celebration and fellowship. But it's reversed. What could that mean?

THE ENERGY OF THE CARD IS EMERGING

You're anticipating or planning a gathering. You can almost taste it.

THE ENERGY OF THE CARD IS RECEDING

The glow of a recent gathering is still with you as you remember it.

THE ENERGY OF THE CARD IS BLOCKED

You feel the need for more 3 of Cups energy in your life, and you feel its absence.

THE ENERGY OF THE CARD APPEARS TO BE HAPPENING BUT, IN REALITY, ISN'T

It's a party, but no one's having fun.

THE ENERGY OF THE CARD REALLY IS HAPPENING BUT APPEARS NOT TO BE

It's an ordeal, but everyone's enjoying themselves.

YOU ARE TRYING TO ACHIEVE THE ENERGY OF THE CARD

You miss your friends, so you call them up to make a lunch date.

THE ENERGY OF THE CARDS IS LATENT

Another aspect of something being hidden, as opposed to apparent, is that it might simply be a potential you have to act on in some way to bring out. For example, what is the latent potential of the 3 of Cups? Consider this: you would like to see your friends, but the opportunity to see them is latent rather than explicit. You might have to do something to get together; you might need to schedule something or call them or text them or whatever to make something happen—it's not just going to happen on its own.

THE ENERGY OF THE CARD IS INTERNAL, NOT EXTERNAL

You are spending the day alone, but you find yourself thinking about how much you love your friends. That is, it's something you're feeling rather than something you're experiencing outside.

Or suppose you're not actually at a party, but you're thinking about the pleasure of being with your friends.

THE ENERGY OF THE CARD IS UNCONSCIOUS, NOT CONSCIOUS

Because we're talking about the unconscious, this is kind of hard to explain. But remember when we talked about "minors as moods" in chapter 2? Even though you are doing your taxes, you are totally grooving to some earworm you have no awareness of having. Later, you wonder why you were enjoying yourself so much. You're in a party kind of mood, but it's completely below your own radar—you're grooving away in your seat, even though you're just at your desk, in your home office. Maybe you're doing some incredibly boring task but you feel really cheerful for no obvious reason.

THE ENERGY OF THE CARD IS THERE, BUT YOU ARE CONFLICTED ABOUT IT

You know you should socialize more, but you just don't feel like it. Maybe you feel like you should see your friends more, but on the other hand you'd rather stay home and watch Netflix. This is a perfectly reasonable point of view. That kind of tug-of-war happens inside all of us all the time.

And, finally, there is one more possibility…

THE READER IS TIRED!

I draw two Cards of the Day every day. When they both come up reversed, it often turns out that I'm just tired. I didn't get enough sleep, or maybe I'm under the weather; my energy is low. It's a signal that I might need to take a nap or do something to raise my vitality enough to get the full benefit of the cards. Perhaps this will be true for you as well.

———

Reversals allow you to read those transitional, conflicted, ambiguous energies and do something constructive with them when you're reading for yourself or others. Often—maybe even most of the time—a person's story is not as straightforward as an upright reading would suggest. As you absorb more context, reversals can help you understand where the gray areas are. They can show you where the potentials are for changing or altering or manipulating the circumstances.

If you decide to use reversals, give the following worksheet a try. I've chosen three different cards for you to read in reversal, but you can choose three different ones if you'd like. It really doesn't matter; it's just a way of developing your reversal muscles.

Don't be afraid of reversals! If they work for you, use them. If they don't, don't worry about it. If you draw a card reversed, you can always just go ahead and turn it upright. That is the beauty of reading a reversal as nuanced rather than as the opposite of itself. There is always the potential to bring out the best in whatever card you get. That's a choice—and when we get to chapter 8, we'll talk a lot more about that choice.

Emerging	You're anticipating or planning a gathering. You can almost taste it.
Receding	The glow of a recent gathering is still with you as you remember it.
Blocked	You feel the need for more social time in your life, and you feel its absence.
Apparent	It's a party, but no one's having fun.
Hidden	It's an ordeal, but everyone's secretly enjoying themselves.
Latent	You miss your friends, so you call them up to make a lunch date.
Internal	You are spending the day alone, but you find yourself thinking about how much you love your friends.
Unconscious	Even though you are just doing your taxes, you are totally grooving in your seat to a tune that's completely in your mind. Later, you wonder why you were enjoying yourself so much.
Conflicted	You know you should socialize more, but you just don't feel like it.

Emerging	
Receding	
Blocked	
Apparent	
Hidden	
Latent	
Internal	
Unconscious	
Conflicted	

Emerging	
Receding	
Blocked	
Apparent	
Hidden	
Latent	
Internal	
Unconscious	
Conflicted	

Emerging	
Receding	
Blocked	
Apparent	
Hidden	
Latent	
Internal	
Unconscious	
Conflicted	

four
THIS I BELIEVE

"This I believe." Why have a chapter on tarot philosophy? Why can't we just read the cards and not worry about the belief structure that lies underneath that? Well, the reason is that tarot is a really powerful tool. It's a tool that can change your life in ways you can't begin to comprehend. It can rearrange the substructure of your outlook on the world, bringing it into focus in the same way a new pair of glasses does. So we ought to have a sense of what's going on in that substructure, that armature of belief we all wear without even being conscious of it. As Carl Jung said, "Until you make the unconscious conscious, it will direct your life and you will call it fate."

Your Tarot Worldview

What are your beliefs about the way the world works, and how do they look in tarot? When we generalize about our world, we tell a story we want to live by. And if we can recognize these assumptions, we can change them. By changing them, we change the story we're living in.

Since the beginning of this book, we've been talking about tarot as kind of a language. The first things we pick up when we're learning a language are the basics of life: how to get around, where we are, who are the people around us. Who, what, where, when, how—in other words, the easy stuff.

But when you become more fluent in a language, that's when you can start to ask hard questions—especially the hardest question of all: *Why?* Now that you speak more fluent tarot, we can look at some of the conceptual structures that lie beneath the way you look at the world: your attitudes, your beliefs, your hang-ups, your demons, and also the better angels of your nature—in other words, *why* you are who you are and *why* you do the things you do. If you can become familiar with these hidden structures that govern your life, then you can also change them.

Everything you believe corresponds to a tarot card in one way or another. Even your doubts have a tarot card. Even (and this is very meta) your doubts *about tarot* have a tarot card! Tarot works as a tool to externalize and work with parts of yourself.

It's a bit like evocation if you're a ceremonial magician. Evocation is a ritual where you externalize a part of yourself and ask it to behave in a particular way. We can argue about whether that spirit you evoke is actually external or not, but it doesn't really matter. Either way, the results will be the same.

How do we get at our assumptions about the world? How do we even begin to recognize what they are so that we can change them? Doesn't it seem as though most of the time we just kind of go through life on autopilot? We act according to what we believe about the world, but we don't often really examine our beliefs. They're just sort of there, and we take them for granted.

Where do they come from? It's a good question. They come from other people—our parents, our family, their values that we've internalized. They come from our lived experience—the things we've learned in school, the lessons life has taught us. And they come from our internal worlds—what we've read or taken into our imaginations.

You'll sometimes notice your beliefs about the world surface when you're talking to your friends or loved ones. For example, suppose you read a newspaper article about a politician misusing campaign funds to buy a personal yacht. You shake your head and say, "That just ain't right!" You've just expressed an opinion about a value. When something like that happens, take note of it and try to figure out what drives that. Is it because you believe people should act fairly toward other people? Is it because you believe everybody gets an equal opportunity? Is it because you believe that hard work deserves recognition?

Sometimes you'll catch yourself expressing beliefs that are probably not even all that helpful—for example, suppose one morning you let someone cut in front of you when you're getting your coffee, and that makes you late to work. You sigh and think, *Nice guys finish last!*

That's something you may not actually really believe, but it's still floating around your head, shaping your perspective of the day.

So when you find yourself making a broad generalization (and you needn't feel bad about that, we all do it), pay attention to what you're saying. Ask yourself if it really has to be true, because our beliefs about the world are actually quite negotiable—it's just that we don't always see them clearly enough to grapple with them.

A Proposed Model of Reality

In this chapter, we're talking about the way symbols turn into reality. This transformation from symbolic to real happens lots of different ways, when you think about it. It might be the images in a proverb ("The early bird gets the worm!"), prompting us to set our alarm for sunrise. It might be the dream about losing the car keys, prompting you to think about security and update your antivirus software the next day. It might be the archetypal figures who inspire us and inhabit our imaginations, causing us to project their images into the outer world ("Gandalf for President!" read the famous bumper sticker from the '70s). It's similar with tarot: when we read the image language of the cards, something subtly shifts in the way we perceive our waking world.

My own belief is that working with symbol, ultimately, is working with reality. That's what makes tarot such a powerful practice. As above, so below; as within, so without. We reflect the larger patterns of the universe, and the universe reflects the patterns within us. One does not precede or cause the other; they co-arise. When we do divination, we deliberately create chaos through randomness or shuffling or scattering. We use that chaotic field to reflect or project the patterns we cannot otherwise perceive. And when that happens, meaningful coincidences between the internal and external reality arise—not sometimes, but *always*. It's what Jung called "synchronicity."

I think that tarot images show us something truthful about our experience, whether we are asking about our past, our present, or our future; when it's our future, we call it divination. They show us the "quality of the moment"; the subtle shape or pattern of things to come, not necessarily the exact thing itself. (Except, of course, for when they actually do show the exact thing itself, like when you draw the 5 of Pentacles and it snows.) To work with tarot is to call forth coincidence, to inhabit the pattern.

If the coincidences we summon don't appear to us to be meaningful, it's not because they aren't. It's because it's up to us to discover the meaning for ourselves, just as when we read a poem it's up to us to uncover what it has to offer; the poet never forces it on us. The word "metaphor" comes from the Greek μεταφέρω, to "apply" or "transfer."[10] We are always responsible for "the last mile" (to borrow a phrase from the telecom industry); it's always up to us to bring the meaning over the finish line.

When we work with tarot, whether as diviners or magicians, we live the poem. We make our dreams reality.

Chapter 4 Assignments: An Overview

In this chapter's assignments, we're going to try and find ways to put words to your belief structure. For the major arcana, we're going to take a bunch of well-known proverbs and see if we can match them to those twenty-two cards. For the minor arcana, we're going to use quotes from actual people. And then we're going to make up our own proverbs, because why not?

Next—in the only exercise in this chapter that doesn't use any tarot cards at all—we're going to take a moment to figure out who's on the other end of the line when we do a reading. We're going to take a close look at the composite structure of our best self, where the angels of our nature reside and can offer their strength and support in a reading. And then, having met and embraced the angels of our nature, we're going to confront our demons.

The first five exercises in this chapter are about talking the talk. But in the last one, we'll walk the walk and deliberately enact what we see in the card. As I said just a moment ago, we will *live the poem*. And that, my friend, is what I mean by magic.

---

10 | S.v. "metaphor," Wiktionary, updated September 4, 2022, https://en.wiktionary.org/wiki/metaphor.

Assignment 4.1

Major Arcana: Proverbs

It's not the easiest thing in the world to know what your own beliefs are (never mind articulating them). So we're going to start by working with other people's beliefs, and a good place to find other people's beliefs is in proverbs. Effective proverbs are just opinions that have been around so long nobody knows who said them. They sound so persuasive that nobody thinks to challenge them. In fact, a lot of them are statements we internalized at a very young age.

In this exercise, we're going to turn proverbs into tarot language. I've chosen a wide variety of proverbs you can assign to the major arcana. There are no "right" answers—every one of us sees the world a bit differently. Please feel free to change the proverbs I've given and hunt for proverbs I haven't until you find something that works for each of these cards. You'll end up with more than one for some cards, and for others you may struggle to find even one that fits. All of this is good—we're learning to wrangle big ideas into figurative language. It's the process itself that's important here.

Once you're done, you'll have a bit more insight into the nature of the card and how it links up with your own belief system.

Instructions

1 | Spread out the twenty-two major arcana cards somewhere you can see all of them at once.

2 | Match each proverb to the major arcana card you think best expresses it. Don't worry if you end up with more than one proverb for each card—that's interesting, and tells you something about the complex nature of these images.

Remember, there are no right answers! And you should feel free to add any additional proverbs you can think of that resonate—or for that matter, that don't!—with your worldview.

"Two wrongs don't make a right."

"The pen is mightier than the sword."

"When in Rome, do as the Romans do."

"The squeaky wheel gets the grease."

"When the going gets tough, the tough get going."

"No man is an island."

"Fortune favors the bold."

"People who live in glass houses should not throw stones."

"Hope for the best, but prepare for the worst."

"Better late than never."

"Birds of a feather flock together."

"Keep your friends close and your enemies closer."

"A picture is worth a thousand words."

"There's no such thing as a free lunch."

"There's no place like home."

"Discretion is the greater part of valor."

"The early bird gets the worm."

"Never look a gift horse in the mouth."

"You can't make an omelet without breaking a few eggs."

"God helps those who help themselves."

"You can't always get what you want."

"Cleanliness is next to godliness."

"A watched pot never boils."

"Beggars can't be choosers."

"Actions speak louder than words."

"If it ain't broke, don't fix it."

"Practice makes perfect."

"Too many cooks spoil the broth."

"Easy come, easy go."

"Don't bite the hand that feeds you."

"All good things must come to an end."

"If you can't beat 'em, join 'em."

"One man's trash is another man's treasure."

"There's no time like the present."

"Beauty is in the eye of the beholder."

"Necessity is the mother of invention."

"A penny saved is a penny earned."

"Familiarity breeds contempt."

"You can't judge a book by its cover."

"Good things come to those who wait."

"Don't put all your eggs in one basket."

"Two heads are better than one."

"The grass is always greener on the other side of the hill."

"Do unto others as you would have them do unto you."

"A chain is only as strong as its weakest link."

"Honesty is the best policy."

"Absence makes the heart grow fonder."

"You can lead a horse to water, but you can't make him drink."

"Don't count your chickens before they hatch."

"If you want something done right, you have to do it yourself."

"One person's meat is another's poison."

"Laugh and the world laughs with you."

"A fish in the hand is worth two in the sea."

"Handsome is as handsome does."

"Slow and steady wins the race."

"Pride comes before a fall."

"United we stand, divided we fall."

"Physician, heal thyself."

"One swallow does not make a summer."

"Look before you leap."

"A house divided against itself cannot stand."

"An eye for an eye, a tooth for a tooth."

"As you sow, so shall you reap."

"Ashes to ashes, dust to dust."

"Blessed are the meek, for they shall inherit the earth."

"Do as I say, not as I do."

"Eat, drink, and be merry, for tomorrow we die."

"For everything there is a season."

"He who lives by the sword dies by the sword."

"How the mighty have fallen."

"It is easier for a camel to go through the eye of a needle than for a rich man to enter into the kingdom of God."

"It's better to give than to receive."

"Love of money is the root of all evil."

"Man does not live by bread alone."

"Many are called, but few are chosen."

"My cup runneth over."

"No rest for the wicked."

"Out of the mouths of babes."

"This too shall pass."

"Render to Caesar the things that are Caesar's."

"The blind leading the blind."

"The spirit is willing, but the flesh is weak."

"There's a time and a place for everything."

"Let he who is without sin cast the first stone."

"You have been weighed in the balances and found wanting!"

Assignment 4.2

Minor Arcana: Quotations

For the minor arcana, we'll be working with quotations from actual people. You may be wondering, *What's the difference between a quotation and a proverb?* That's a good question. I think it's possible quotations are really just proverbs in the making—opinions that are recent enough that we actually know who said them. They also seem to me to be a bit more specific and contextualized than the proverbs we explored in the previous exercise. Because quotations are so relatable and the people who said them are known quantities, they seem to be a good fit with the minor arcana, which express our everyday lived experiences.

Instructions

1 | Spread out your Ace through 10 minor arcana (forty cards total) so you can see them all.

2 | Match the following quotes to the minor card you think best corresponds to it.

3 | There will be at least eighteen cards that don't have quotes when you're done. Find quotes for each of the remaining cards. These can be from any source you like: print, television, radio, YouTube, TikTok. It's also fine to use quotes from non-famous people, like your gran, or your high school biology teacher, or the foulmouthed barista at your local Starbucks. You can even quote yourself, if you've got a good one you're known for saying!

"I have stood on a mountain of no's for one yes." —B. Smith

"I do believe that if you haven't learnt about sadness, you cannot appreciate happiness." —Nana Mouskouri

"Courage is resistance to fear, mastery of fear, not absence of fear." —Mark Twain

"Some people go to priests; others to poetry; I to my friends." —Virginia Woolf

"Grief is in two parts. The first is loss. The second is the remaking of life." —Anne Roiphe

"Winning isn't everything, but it beats anything in second place." —William C. Bryant

"Half an hour's meditation each day is essential, except when you are busy. Then a full hour is needed." —Saint Francis de Sales

"A surplus of effort could overcome a deficit of confidence." —Sonia Sotomayor

"Let us always meet each other with a smile, for a smile is the beginning of love." —Mother Teresa

"Choose a job you love, and you will never have to work a day in your life." —Anonymous

"Learn from the mistakes of others. You can't live long enough to make them all yourself." —Eleanor Roosevelt

"Family is not an important thing. It's everything." —Michael J. Fox

"Everything changes and nothing stands still." —Heraclitus

"If you don't like the road you're walking, start paving another one." —Dolly Parton

"Step out of the history that is holding you back. Step into the new story you are willing to create." —Oprah

"Enough is as good as a feast." —Anonymous

"Optimism is the faith that leads to achievement." —Helen Keller

"Anyone who has struggled with poverty knows how extremely expensive it is to be poor." —James Baldwin

"Patience is not simply the ability to wait—it's how we behave while we're waiting." —Joyce Meyer

"I tend to get bored quickly, which means I must be boring." —Anthony Hopkins

"Do not be anxious about tomorrow, for tomorrow will be anxious for itself." —Jesus Christ

"First they ignore you, then they laugh at you, then they fight you, then you win." —Mahatma Gandhi

_____   _____   _____   _____   _____

_____   _____   _____   _____   _____

_____   _____   _____   _____   _____

_____   _____   _____   _____   _____

———————   ———————   ———————   ———————   ———————

———————   ———————   ———————   ———————   ———————

———————   ———————   ———————   ———————   ———————

———————   ———————   ———————   ———————   ———————

Assignment 4.3

DIY Proverbs

In this exercise, you're going to draw six cards at random and make up a proverb for each of them. This is a little bit like the Tarot Forward exercises that we did in the last chapter and a little bit like a creative writing exercise.

You're going to look at your six cards, one at a time, and make a generalized statement out of each of them. Try to use the images in the card as a basis for your proverb. For example:

"Hands that gather roses can tame lions!"

"Those who chain themselves are their own worst demons."

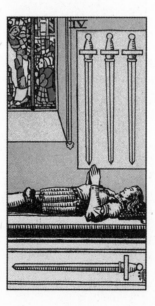

"Life goes on just the same while heroes sleep."

They don't need to make a ton of sense, and they don't need to be literally true. You also don't need to actually believe it. Regardless, what you come up with will likely be quite revealing of the way you look at the world, and perhaps you'll have a better idea of the forces and influences that might be informing your readings. If you like, you can test your proverbs on a friend who's fluent in tarot to see if they can identify the cards.

Play around with it! And prepare to be surprised by what you see in tarot's mirror.

Instructions

1 | Draw six cards at random.

2 | Make up a proverb for each of them based on the symbols and imagery you see in each card. Try to make it sound like it's something people have said for ages.

———

1 | Card I Drew: _____

Proverb: _____

2 | Card I Drew: _____

Proverb: _____

3 | Card I Drew: _____

Proverb: _____

4 | Card I Drew: _____

Proverb: _____

5 | Card I Drew: _____

Proverb: _____

6 | Card I Drew: _____

Proverb: _____

Assignment 4.4

Who You Gonna Call?

In this assignment—which is kind of for fun, but also kind of serious—we're going to think about who's on "the other end" when you're doing a tarot reading. It's a good question, isn't it? There are lots of people in this world who consciously avoid tarot. For the most part they divide into those who think you *can't* do it (i.e., how can it possibly work, in a rational world?) and those who think you *shouldn't* do it. Of those who think you shouldn't do it, it's often because they feel fearful that we might be channeling demons or malevolent spirits. I've even had people ask me, "Isn't it satanic?"

If you're reading this book, my guess is that you, like me, don't believe tarot is the least bit satanic. Nevertheless, I think it's a good idea to ask *who's on the other end* when you're talking to tarot. Since we mostly turn to tarot for advice (or at least a good idea, or a shift in perspective), we can approach that the same way we do in real life. If you wanted advice or good ideas or a shift in perspective in real life, you'd call your mom or your best friend or a mentor. You wouldn't want to just ask some random troll you met on the internet, and you definitely wouldn't ask your mean uncle who makes you feel terrible about yourself.

The way I see it, a tarot deck is like a phone: it's a tool, a communication device. You get to decide who you call. It's not like you just pick up the phone and listen to whoever's on the line. But if you don't decide who you're gonna call, well, it could kind of be like that. You could get anybody—meaning, you could get any random thoughts that are floating around in your head, including ones that are not particularly helpful. We've all had moments when our very worst impulses come out of the woodwork and say things like *You're a loser* or *You can't do anything* or *You always make mistakes.* This is, needless to say, unhelpful.

So when we ask *Who's on the other end?* in a tarot reading, I usually tell people to think of the person on the other end as the best version of themselves: in other words, you as your own best friend. In this exercise, we're going to break that down a little further, because I believe that our own best selves don't just emerge from a vacuum. I think they're kind of an amalgam of the best qualities people have projected onto us, plus things that inspire us: values we believe in, aspirations we may have.

In this exercise, we're going to try and identify those qualities and beliefs, those most powerful forces for good in your life. We're going to name them, we're going to talk about them, and then we're going to come up with a way of calling on them when you sit down to do a tarot reading. You're going to think about the good feelings you get when you think about these characters or versions of yourself or qualities that people believe you have. When you're feeling at your strongest, that's when you do the reading. This is how you structurally encourage messages from tarot that help you create positive change in your life—change you can believe in. Because if you find yourself stewing over a reading and thinking, *These are just some negative thoughts spiraling around in my head that tarot is reflecting back to me*—well, that really doesn't do you any good at all, does it?

By the end of this assignment you're going to have some kind of verbal statement of belief or invocation—a credo, if you like—that you can use as something to say when you start reading. But the more important thing is the *feeling* that you get from it. Remember in *Harry Potter and the Prisoner of Azkaban* when Harry learns the Patronus charm? He's asked to think of the happiest memory he has, and that memory acts as a shield against the powers of evil, which in the Potterverse take the form of Dementors. When you do a tarot reading, you're casting a Patronus charm. You want to find that place inside you where you are strong, happy, self-supporting, and capable. Because tarot is special—it's magical, and you don't want to just throw away this incredibly powerful moment that occurs every time you pick up a tarot deck.

Put yourself in the right frame of mind. Take it seriously, and you'll get out of it what you put into it.

Instructions

Here's a list of questions that will help you locate, identify, and recognize your own best self when it's speaking. Try to focus on figures you care about and know a lot about. For example, I super-admire Papa Legba, but since I don't know his tradition well, he's not an aspect of myself I think I can call on. Are your mentors, guides, and gods external to you or internal? Some people think this matters. Personally, I don't see why it should. Can't they be both? Myself, I tend to think we're connecting with what Jung might have called the archetypal Self—that illuminated constellation that spans and unites the conscious, unconscious, and collective realms within us.

Write down your answers in your journal, on your device, or right here in this workbook. Make sure you know how to find this list in the future and update as necessary.

1 | What do your parents, family, and close friends love most about you?

_____

_____

_____

2 | Who are the real-life people you know whom you really like to ask for advice?

_____

_____

_____

3 | Who are the real-life people you don't know whom you would really like to ask for advice (can include prominent figures, e.g., Barack Obama or the Dalai Lama, or even deceased people)?

_____

_____

_____

4 | Who are the imaginary people and natural spirits whom you would really like to ask for advice (the neighborhood oak tree, Dumbledore, Galadriel, the Pacific Ocean, etc.)?

_____

_____

_____

5 | Who are the gods whom you would really like to ask for advice?

_____

_____

_____

6 | Finally, make up a short invocation or statement of belief calling on the specific characters or qualities you've mentioned above. Just a few sentences is fine. It can be in second person ("I call on you, Spirit, wise as Gandalf and patient as Atlas!") or in first person ("I am infinitely kind and full of insight! I am resourceful and full of hope!") *Note: You are only going to have to believe this for short stretches at a time.*

_____

_____

_____

● ● ● ● ● ● ●

Assignment 4.5

Self-Talk Assignment

Folks, this one's going to take you places. So *make sure* you've done the previous exercise, "Who You Gonna Call?" before beginning this one. If you're like me, you're probably going in order through this book anyway. But if you aren't, take a little time to do Assignment 4.4 before proceeding. Okay?

The Self-Talk Assignment is a form of shadow work. Please go slowly and be gentle with yourself. If you start to feel upset or despairing, or overwhelmed by negative thoughts, stop and set it aside for a bit. In this exercise, we're going to take a look at some of your personal demons, and then we're going to work with them.

You'll start by spreading out the entire deck so you can see it, and then we'll start externalizing our demons. For example: maybe you have the demon of believing that you're a terrible friend. It's not the worst demon in the world, but it does bother a lot of us, so see if you can find a card that represents that. I could give you some suggestions, but I think it's better that you go through the tarot deck and figure it out for yourself. Know that there *is* a card that can represent that for you, even if it's pretty approximate. When you've found that card, you're going to ask yourself, *What is it saying to me?* Give it a voice; express what it's saying in a sentence or two, and enter that in the left-hand column.

Then you're going to look at that card and remind yourself that every card has a positive side and a negative side (see Assignment 1.2). Sometimes the negative side is nothing more than a positive side that's gotten imbalanced or gone a little bit out of whack somehow. Each of these cards has a function, and even the toughest ones are not there to plague you and make life a living hell. They're there because they're tools in the toolbox of human experience. Take the terribly anxious 9 of Swords, for example; anxiety has an evolutionary purpose, which is to protect us from dangerous things by allowing us to anticipate them. So in this step, you're trying to pinpoint the useful function of that card rather than just pushing it away, and you'll write that down in the middle column of the chart.

Finally, you're going to choose one more card—not a random card, but a deliberately chosen one based on what you think would be an appropriate choice as a positive response. This card will represent a good way of dealing with the negative energy of the first card. If you have trouble finding it at first, access that positive, helpful, wise version of yourself we met in the last exercise and ask, *What's your best advice for dealing with this?* Once you've found it, you're going to give the card a voice—a response to the negative things you wrote in the first column. You're going to let this card literally have the last word.

Needless to say, this is a very powerful exercise. Choose your last card very carefully. Make it something you can believe in. And when you find yourself experiencing negative self-talk in the days ahead, you're going to be able to go back to this chart and ask, *What is my best response to that?* Sometimes you're just going to remember what the card looks like and that's going to be enough. Your response card, in the end, should be more powerful than the card representing the negative thought. Ultimately, this is a balancing-out exercise that, when done properly, will give your better self a louder voice.

Instructions

1 | Spread out your whole tarot deck. Create a five-column structure in your notebook or on your computer.

2 | In column one, write down the narratives you tell yourself. (What memories do you replay? What distracts you? What causes you anxiety? What makes you feel bad about yourself? What discourages you from acting?)

3 | In column two, write down one card that can represent those narratives for you.

4 | In column three, ask yourself what the *positive* side of the card you chose is. (What purpose does it serve? In what way is it an essential part of the human experience? Refer back to Assignment 1.2 if need be.)

5 | Next, choose a card that can represent an ally to help you counter your self-talk. Write down what card it is in column four.

6 | In column five, write down what that card might say on your behalf.

Here's an example to demonstrate what I mean.

1. Negative Self-Talk	2. Self-Talk Card	3. Positive Side of Self-Talk Card	4. Response Card	5. Conscious Response
"Other people have their lives more together than me! Why are they better than me? I suck! Therefore, they suck!"	5 of Swords	"Competitiveness is not all bad. It makes you try harder. You can always compete against yourself."	8 of Pentacles	"You have strong priorities and work hard on the things you care about. That's what matters."

_____

_____

_____

_____

_____

_____

_____

_____

_____

_____

_____

Chapter 4 Final Assignment
Walk the Walk

By now, you've heard me talk quite a lot about "living the poem" when you work with tarot, and for this final assignment we're going to do just that. Rather than simply looking out for the synchronicities and coincidences that tarot draws to our attention, we're going to actively seek out ways to express what's in the card. (This is actually a preview of chapter 8, where we will begin the adventure of changing ourselves and the world around us through the vehicle of tarot.)

Instructions

1 | Draw one card. Over the course of a day, find a way to enact its literal appearance and/ or its symbolic meaning or message. Use the following prompts to help you if you wish. Feel free to find multiple means, modes, and layers of expression!

   • What are the figures depicted on the card doing? What would it look like in your life if you did something like that?

   • What are they wearing? Are their clothes for protection? For courtship? To show status? What clothes do you have that can fulfill that purpose?

   • What's their body language? What would you likely be doing if you were in that stance?

   • What is their facial expression? Their mood? Can you think of a way to put yourself in that state of mind?

   • If the card represented the first moment in a five-minute scene, what would happen next? Can you think of a way to enact that narrative arc in your own day?

   • What are some of the positive and negative meanings of the card? How might you demonstrate that in your life?

2 | Document the experience of enacting the card.

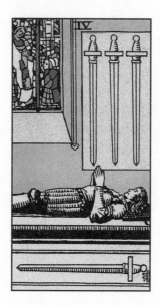

For example, if you drew the 4 of Swords, you might lie down for a nap, fully dressed, like the knight who is the main character in this image. You might kneel in prayer like the figure in the stained glass window. Based on the meaning rather than the literal image, you might take a deep breath in the middle of an argument. You might give your kid a time-out (but only if they deserve it!). You might write down a dream you had last night.

———

• Card I Drew: _____

• Symbolism I Noticed: _____

_____

_____

_____

_____

• How I "Lived the Poem": _____

_____

_____

_____

_____

_____

five
ASK A QUESTION

Can you believe we've gotten halfway through this book and we're only *just now* talking about asking a question? After all, the reason people come to tarot, when it comes right down to it, is *so they can ask questions*.

It may have taken us a while to get here, but we really did have to do the groundwork first. Why? Well, to go back to our language analogy: if you ask a question in a foreign language, how likely are you to understand the answer? You've mastered a few phrases from a book or an app or an instructor, and they gave you the impression you'd get a short one or two sentence reply that you would *totally* understand, and the person would say it *very slowly*, and that would be that. But in reality, answers tend to be a lot more complex than just "Yes" or "No" or "The bathroom is over there, behind the woman in the red jacket." At least, the answers worth having.

Answers in tarot are as complex as they are in life, so you needed to speak the language of tarot with some fluency before you could understand what tarot was trying to say. At first, tarot speaks impressionistically, like "This looks really exciting!" or "This looks very discouraging!" But as our neural map of the cards fills out and complexifies, we find these basic statements take on dimension and nuance, illuminating scenarios, liabilities, and projections we never anticipated.

Asking a question is what draws these visions forth; it is the shout that triggers the echo, the stone that causes the ripples, the sunlight that cracks the seed hull. (There are a few fortunate readers, I should note, who don't need a question to give you a reading; their intuition guides them to simply start talking and tell you what you need to know. But for the vast majority of us, the framing that questions provide is vital.)

So, asking a question is at the heart of tarot, and asking a *good* question matters.

Prediction, Insight—and Agency

I'm going to be bold and say there are two kinds of tarot questions.

The first type of question is *What's going to happen?* i.e., prediction. The second type of question is *Why is this happening?* i.e., insight. Reading for insight is perhaps the favored way of reading tarot these days, but prediction is worth considering too.

In your hopefully long career as a tarot reader, you will probably encounter readers who say they don't do prediction at all. These are what I think of as Question Two readers. That's totally legitimate, and you may ultimately decide you are a Question Two reader as well. But in this workbook, we're going to learn to do both.

But before we get into the nitty gritty of *What's going to happen?* and *Why is this happening?*, there's another question I should mention. It's one that many readers don't address, but that I think might be the most important of all: *What can I do about it?* Because if you don't try and do something with the information that you've gotten from your reading, then you're living out a self-fulfilling prophecy. Something's going to happen, but you no longer have a say in what it is. That's fatalism, and it's the biggest danger we deal with when we declare ourselves to be diviners and turn to face the unknown.

Fate and Free Will

If we are going to try and answer those questions—*What's going to happen? Why is this happening? What can I do about it?*—we have to talk about fate and free will for a moment. (Some people prefer to say "determinism" and "agency.") I believe that we live suspended between those two forces; some things we can't change, and some things we can. Some things we don't want to change, and some things we should. These distinctions become heightened when we work with tarot.

A common belief people have when first coming to tarot is to think that by engaging with tarot, you're simply revealing a destiny that has already been prewritten in its entirety. From this perspective, all you're doing in the reading is getting some inside information. At best, this kind of fatalism confirms what you already believe. At worst, it deprives you of all motivation to do anything at all about your future.

On the other hand (particularly in twenty-first-century America), we're often encouraged to think we can do anything at all if we just put our minds to it. While helpful up to a point, this attitude fails spectacularly when things don't go our way—and sooner or later, we all experience failure of one kind or another. Clearly, we think, it *must* have been our fault. Clearly, we think, we weren't trying hard enough. But really, how does that help us?

In chapter 4, I said that tarot images show us the "quality of the moment"; the subtle shape or pattern of things to come. It's my belief that while the general shape of things to come may be a matter of fate, its specific expression falls much more in the realm of free will.

Here's an astrological analogy: the Saturn return. Around age twenty-nine, you might make the decision to take on more responsibility when it comes to adulting. If you don't, you might find you are forced to face responsibility in a way that is less subjectively welcome than the conscious choice to do so would have been. The other analogy I like is automotive: you're far less likely to experience motion sickness when you're in the driver's seat than when you're just sitting on the passenger side looking at your phone. In both cases, the circumstances remain the same. But your experience of them may be vastly different.

In truth, I think neither fate nor free will works quite the way we think they do, and we may never have a perfect model for that. However, bearing that in mind, I've found that the following way of looking at the world works quite well:

It is constructive to use your illusion of free will to deal with your illusion of fate.

In other words: Sure, there may be limits to what you can do (magicians I know like to give this example: "As much as I would like to, I cannot be a pro basketball player because I'm only five foot seven!"). But if you *act like* you live in a free will universe, you're likely to find you can do a lot more than you think. There are rules to this game of life, but that doesn't mean you can't play. You can, and you should.

Using the Map

It's good to remember that tarot is not, in itself, a god or a demon. It can feel like a spiritual entity, and maybe it is. Sometimes it's fun to think of it as having a personality. But when it comes right down to it, it's healthy to think of tarot as more like a vehicle, or a tool, or an apparatus. A spooky and sacred one, to be sure, and worthy of respect and special treatment. But ultimately, you're the one calling the shots, not the cards.

My favorite analogy for tarot is the map analogy. What does a map do? It gives you information. It tells you how you can get from Point A to Point B. It can tell you what towns are nearby; it can offer you a variety of possible destinations. It can tell you how easy or how hard it is to get to them; it can help you figure out what's reasonable and not reasonable to try and do in a single day. But there is one thing a map does not do: *It does not tell you what you should do.*

With a map, you trace your own journey, wherever it is you mean to go. You could go today, you could go tomorrow, you could go *never*. You could go north, or south, or to the equator if you want. You can travel straight as the crow flies, or you could drive around in circles so that a journey of five miles takes you five days. *You could throw the map out the window.*

That's free will.

When you're working with tarot, ultimately you decide who you're going to talk to and where you're going to go. That's not to say there aren't limits—sometimes circumstances sharply reduce our options. But there is always a better and a worse response to every situation, and tarot helps us figure out what's the better response for us.

Prediction, Insight, and Why You Are Psychic

Asking good questions helps you suss out where the limits of fate fall for you personally, as well as the best responses to those limits. In chapters 1, 2, and 3 you expanded your understanding of what a card can mean so that each card now offers you a reasonably broad range of interpretation. In chapter 4 we asked where the information and advice you receive in a tarot reading is coming from; hopefully, you now trust the "best version of yourself" well enough to listen to it. As anyone who has ever done any kind of divination will tell you, the messages can seem uncanny; weirdly apt; right on target. That's because this expanded version of yourself—your Big Self, if you like—is magical and perceptive, and it knows a whole lot more than you think.

In this chapter, we're taking the Big Self out for a test drive. I've mentioned the concepts of prediction and insight. For the purposes of this chapter's assignment, we're going to call prediction "Looking Far." And we're going to call insight "Looking Deep."

You might be worried you're not intuitive enough for prediction. A lot of people first approaching predictive tarot think, *God, I'm about as psychic as a doorknob. There's no way I'm going to be able to predict anything.* But the fact is, you do have predictive ability—everybody does—because you have pattern-making ability.

This could be as simple as what happens when you throw a ball: you know roughly where it's going to land, thanks to the laws of physics. Now you may say "Well, yeah, but that's physics. That's different." Well, then, let's consider another example. Have you ever been having a conversation with your friend and you know exactly what they're about to say—and then they say it? That is not physics. That is prediction, and everybody can do it to some extent. "Oh, that's just normal," you might say. Well, yes. Pattern-making is normal. Prediction is normal.

Need more examples? Say you've lost your keys. You're hunting all over the place, silently fuming. Then at some point you say, out loud, "Where are my keys?!" and in that moment, you see them. They turn up in a spot where you've literally looked five times. It's almost as if you said a magical spell when you asked where your keys were. And how about breakup songs? If you've ever broken up with someone, you might notice it seems like every single song you hear on the radio or on shuffle is about breaking up. Every single thing is suddenly about you. Funny, isn't it?

Now, you can argue that that's just your brain filtering out everything except what's relevant to you. But isn't that exactly what we're doing in a tarot reading? We are filtering out the information that is not useful to us and making a pattern out of the information that is. It's that simple. So let's set aside your doubts about whether you're psychic, okay? "Psychic" is just a word that gets in the way.

Chapter 5 Assignments: An Overview

The assignments in this chapter—and honestly, the assignments in most of the rest of this book—are journaling assignments. Up to this point, you've been working with concepts and phrases and individual meanings. But now, we are going to see what happens when you put those concepts and phrases and meanings into context—i.e., interpretation. This is the heart of what we do as tarot readers: we build narratives and story trajectories; we tell tales. In fact, in some ways we're not so much readers as *authors*.

These assignments are like the word problems you did in math class, only instead of figuring out how far a locomotive traveling at seventy miles per hour can go in forty-three minutes, you're going to try and figure out what is going to happen next to each of the people in several hypothetical scenarios. Also, while the right answer to the locomotive question is *about fifty miles*, in these exercises there are no right or wrong answers. As long as you can come up with a rationale for what you said that makes sense to you, you're good.

Just for fun, I decided to name most of the characters after the Golden Dawn–adjacent individuals whose decks were responsible for launching the modern era of tarot: McGregor Mathers, Pamela Colman Smith, Aleister Crowley, Arthur Edward Waite, Frieda Harris, etc. The names are real; the situations, while plausible, are fictional. Your answers cannot harm anyone! You'll be using the Backward Tarot technique you first learned in chapter 2—coming up with cards that best describe each scenario. Eventually, of course, you will draw the cards randomly, but right now we're choosing them deliberately.

Expect to write a paragraph or two for these kinds of assignments, because you'll need at least a few sentences to describe the card you got, the meaning that suggested itself to you, and why that meaning is relevant for the circumstance. (Needless to say, more is always fine.)

The first two exercises are "Look Far," predictive exercises based on hypothetical scenarios happening to other people. The second two exercises are "Look Deep" insight-based exercises, looking at what happens when you extend those scenarios further. All four of these exercises test your capacity for empathy; all four challenge you to imagine yourself in someone else's life, which is a skill you will use every day of your life as a tarot reader.

And in your final assignment for this chapter, you turn to a problem or concern of your own. You use the skills you just practiced to come up with some possible outcomes and interpretations, and finally—to the sound of angelic harps and victorious trumpets!—you draw your card and find your answer.

Assignment 5.1

Look Far: What Is Likely to Happen?

In this first assignment, I describe for you the nature of the problem at hand, both in words and with a tarot card. Then I posit three possible outcomes. (You're certainly welcome to devise additional outcomes if you like.) For each of these outcomes, you're going to decide which card best represents it; i.e., you're choosing a card *deliberately* rather than drawing *randomly*. (It's a way of applying the tarot language you developed in the first half of the book.) You may end up having a few different candidates for each of these options. You only get to choose one, so take your time and narrow it down to your single best card, and then explain why you chose it.

I encourage you to think of these characters as real people (although they are not), and to bring a nonjudgmental, compassionate spirit to the exercise. We are all human; we are all flawed, and we could all use someone to listen and help, if they can.

Instructions

What do the possible outcomes of each of these scenarios look like in tarot? Name one card for each and, in a few sentences, explain why you chose it. Was there a connection in the imagery? The mood? A keyword or correspondence?

Scenario 1: Pam's Problem

Pam is married. While on a trip, she had a one-night fling with a coworker. Let's call this situation the 7 of Swords. What is likely to happen?

1 | It never happens again and Pam never mentions it to her husband, who never suspects a thing.

• Card I Chose: _____

• Why I Chose This Card: _____

_____

_____

_____

_____

2 | The fling develops into a thing. Pam feels deeply conflicted and begins to wonder if she should leave her marriage.

   • Card I Chose: _____

   • Why I Chose This Card: _____

_____

_____

_____

3 | Pam talks about it with her therapist, who advises her to talk it over with her husband and offers a couples counseling referral.

   • Card I Chose: _____

   • Why I Chose This Card: _____

_____

_____

_____

Scenario 2: Aleister's Dilemma

Aleister is sick of his job at Starbucks—really sick of it. He dreams of going back to school, or maybe trying to make it as a musician. Let's call this situation the 4 of Cups. What is likely to happen?

1 | Aleister does nothing. He keeps working at the Starbucks, but he complains to his friend Pam a lot.

   • Card I Chose: _____

   • Why I Chose This Card: _____

   _____

   _____

   _____

2 | Aleister starts researching grad school. He requests his transcripts and asks for recommendations from his old professors. He's still not sure. He wonders if he can handle work and school.

   • Card I Chose: _____

   • Why I Chose This Card: _____

   _____

   _____

   _____

3 | One day Aleister just up and quits his job. He moves back in with his folks while he decides what to do.

- Card I Chose: _____

- Why I Chose This Card: _____

  _____

  _____

  _____

Scenario 3: Arthur's Identity Crisis

Arthur has just retired, and he doesn't know what to do with himself. He's at home, he's bored, he's driving his spouse crazy, and he feels sort of worthless. Let's call this situation the Judgement card. What is likely to happen?

1 | Arthur is watching a lot of YouTube. He notices a DIY video that tells you how to fix a leaky faucet. He realizes there are a lot of things around the house that could use some attention.

- Card I Chose: _____

- Why I Chose This Card: _____

  _____

  _____

2 | Arthur indulges himself in all the relaxing things he used to do to unwind. He parks himself in front of the game with a beer. His armchair develops a deep sag in the seat because he's sitting there so much. He gains ten pounds.

- Card I Chose: _____

- Why I Chose This Card: _____

_____

_____

_____

3 | Arthur has more time to read, so he walks to the library a lot. He exhausts the collection pretty quickly, but he notices he enjoys seeing people from his town there.

- Card I Chose: _____

- Why I Chose This Card: _____

_____

_____

_____

Assignment 5.2

Look Far: What "Should" I Do?
(or, What Is Likely to Happen If...?)

In your first Look Far assignment you asked, "What is going to happen?" In this one, you're going to address the natural follow-up question: What "should" I do?

I've put "should" in scare quotes because I think it's a little problematic. When you think *What should I do?*, the question always remains: *According to whom?* Hopefully, because you've already read chapter 4, the answer is now something along the lines of "According to the best version of myself"—i.e., the very best amalgamation of influences in your life; your guides, your gods, your spirits, your mentors, everything and everyone who has your best interests at heart.

However, if you're reading for someone else (or if you're reading for yourself in a rush), you probably haven't gone through that process. When the person across from you asks, "What should I do?" you don't know whether they mean "What do my parents think I should do?" or "What do my peers think I should do?" or "What do you, tarot reader, think I should do?" So I often prefer to just take "should" completely out of the equation.

Fortunately, it's very easy to quickly rephrase a "should" question, and one way to do that is to turn it into a predictive, Look Far question. Instead of asking "What should I do?" in a completely open-ended way, we come up with some options: *What is likely to happen if I do A? B? C?*

Essentially, we're taking the predictive question "What is likely to happen?" and adding "if" to it. This conditional or hypothetical thinking takes us one step further away from reality as given and one step further into the realm of possible futures.

When working with hypotheticals, I find it's best not to go too far. One step is good; five or six steps starts to get you into a linear, passive headspace, which is the opposite of what we want. So, "What is likely to happen if I contact my ex?" is a fair question. But you're gonna make yourself crazy if you start thinking like this: *If I contact my ex via email, what is likely to happen if I start "Dear John"? versus "Hey"? versus "Just thinking of you"?* Just don't.

Instructions

1 | For each of these problems, I've highlighted one of the answers from Assignment 5.1. Look up the card you chose to describe that answer, and set that card aside.

2 | Now that you have the answer to what was going to happen, your client—Pamela, Aleister, or Arthur—is asking "What should I do?" i.e., "What is likely to happen if I…" Imagine three possible answers—three different hypothetical paths the client might take. What cards might represent these three possible answers?

   For example, in the case of the first scenario, Pam's Problem, we're going to pretend that outcome two has happened. Pam's fling has developed into an affair; she is feeling conflicted and doesn't know what to do. She asks you, "What should I do?" Your job is to come up with three possible approaches. For example, she could leave her husband; she could go to therapy and try and work it out; she could carry on trying to manage both relationships. There are other possibilities, obviously, but that's a few off the top of my head. For each possible path, think of a card that represents it. Write these three possible answers down; no need to pull the actual cards.

3 | Then, having decided what those possible paths are and which cards represent them, you're going to shuffle the deck and draw JUST ONE card randomly. This card will likely not be one of the three cards that you imagined. If it is, great! But if it isn't, that's good too. You've now started thinking from the point of view of your client, and you should be able to interpret whatever card it is according to the situation.

Scenario 1: Pam's Problem

Pam is married. She has had a one-night fling with a coworker while on a trip. The fling has developed into a thing, and now Pam is feeling conflicted. Pam asks, "What should I do?"

- What card did you choose to describe this scenario in Assignment 5.1? Set it aside.
- Rephrase the "should" question. What can Pam do about it? What will happen if…?

   - New Question: _____

• Imagine three possible paths. What three cards could represent these paths? (There is no need to remove the actual cards from your deck; this is an imaginative exercise.)

    • Path One: _____

    • Representing Card: _____

    • Path Two: _____

    • Representing Card: _____

    • Path Three: _____

    • Representing Card: _____

• Shuffle the deck, leaving aside only the card describing the original scenario. Randomly draw one card. What does it signify, and what's your advice to Pam?

    • Random Card: _____

    • My Interpretation: _____

    _____

    _____

    _____

    _____

    • Advice I'd Give Pam: _____

    _____

    _____

    _____

    _____

Scenario 2: Aleister's Dilemma

Aleister is sick of his job at Starbucks. He dreams of going back to school, or maybe trying to make it as a musician. One day he just up and quits his job. He moves back in with his folks while he decides what to do. Aleister asks, "What should I do?"

- What card did you choose to describe this scenario in Assignment 5.1? Set it aside.

- Rephrase the "should" question. What can Aleister do about it? What will happen if…?

  - New Question: _____

- Imagine three possible paths. What three cards could represent these paths? (There is no need to remove the actual cards from your deck; this is an imaginative exercise.)

  - Path One: _____

  - Representing Card: _____

  - Path Two: _____

  - Representing Card: _____

  - Path Three: _____

  - Representing Card: _____

- Shuffle the deck, leaving aside only the card describing the original scenario. Randomly draw one card. What does it signify, and what's your advice to Aleister?

  - Random Card: _____

  - My Interpretation: _____

  _____

  _____

  _____

  _____

• Advice I'd Give Aleister: _____

_____

_____

_____

_____

Scenario 3: Arthur's Identity Crisis

Arthur has just retired, and he doesn't know what to do with himself. He has more time to read, so he walks to the library a lot. He notices he enjoys seeing and chatting with people from his town there. But he's bored, and he feels sort of worthless. Arthur asks, "What should I do?"

• What card did you choose to describe this scenario in Assignment 5.1? Set it aside.

• Rephrase the "should" question. What can Arthur do about it? What will happen if…?

    • New Question: _____

• Imagine three possible paths. What three cards could represent these paths? (There is no need to remove the actual cards from your deck; this is an imaginative exercise.)

    • Path One: _____

    • Representing Card: _____

    • Path Two: _____

    • Representing Card: _____

    • Path Three: _____

    • Representing Card: _____

• Shuffle the deck, leaving aside only the card describing the original scenario. Randomly draw one card. What does it signify, and what's your advice to Arthur?

    • Random Card: _____

    • My Interpretation: _____

    _____

    _____

    _____

    _____

    • Advice I'd Give Arthur: _____

    _____

    _____

    _____

    _____

Assignment 5.3

Look Deep: Why Is X Happening?

With the Look Deep assignments, we turn to an essential approach you'll be using over and over in your tarot practice: cause and effect; the "why" and "how" of things. Whether or not you decide to practice prediction, you'll definitely be working with the question of why things are the way they are. If you can gain some insight into motives and causes, you can establish a narrative trajectory and better understand what story you (or your client) are enacting—as well as how to change it.

As with the first assignment in this chapter, I'm going to give you a situation and a card to represent it. Then we'll look at three possible root causes for how this situation came about. Your job is to come up with a card that represents each of the root causes in the language of tarot. Sometimes the root causes in different problems turn out to be similar, so don't worry if you end up using some of the same cards more than once.

As always, feel free to riff! See if you can come up with some additional root causes and cards that might describe them.

Instructions

What do the possible root causes of each of these scenarios look like in tarot? Name one card for each and, in a few sentences, explain why you chose it. Was there a connection in the imagery? The mood? A keyword or correspondence?

Scenario 1: Frieda's Heartache

Relations are strained between Frieda and her grown son, Harry. He lives nearby, but they haven't talked in months. Let's call this situation the 5 of Pentacles. Why is this happening? What are some of the possible root causes?

What do each of these root causes look like in tarot? Name one card for each and explain why you chose it.

1 | Frieda is disappointed in Harry. She always thought he would be a professional and an achiever, like she is. Instead he has a minimum-wage job and spends his free time gaming with his friends. Harry dislikes feeling judged.

   • Root Cause Card: _____

   • Why I Chose It: _____

   _____

   _____

2 | Frieda and Harry have opposing and firmly held political views. They can't talk without getting into an argument. Each feels disrespected.

   • Root Cause Card: _____

   • Why I Chose It: _____

   _____

   _____

3 | Frieda and Harry's dad divorced a few years ago. Frieda has recently started seeing someone for the first time since the split. This is awkward for everyone.

   • Root Cause Card: _____

   • Why I Chose It: _____

   _____

   _____

Scenario 2: McGregor's Dream

McGregor is having a recurring dream. He is always trying to go somewhere, but something always prevents him—a monster, a wrong turn, he forgot his keys…Let's call this recurring dream situation the Moon. Why is this happening? What are some of the possible root causes?

What do each of these root causes look like in tarot? Name one card for each and explain why you chose it.

THE MOON.

1 | McGregor is undergoing a sexual identity crisis. He is uncomfortable with the new self that is trying to assert itself; he tries to push away his thoughts about it when they arise.

- Root Cause Card: _____

- Why I Chose It: _____

_____

_____

_____

2 | McGregor has been working a long time at his office without a promotion or pay raise. He knows he's worth more, but he is afraid to say something.

- Root Cause Card: _____

- Why I Chose It: _____

_____

_____

3 | When McGregor was young, he was a "good kid." If his parents told him not to do something, he wouldn't do it. Now his parents are not around, and he is starting to yearn for adventure.

- Root Cause Card: _____

- Why I Chose It: _____

_____

_____

Scenario 3: Moina's Novel

Moina wants to write a novel. Every time she sits down to write, though, she gets distracted, or discouraged, or thinks of something more important to do. She never seems to complete more than a few sentences at a time. Let's call this situation the Page of Swords. Why is this happening? What are some of the possible root causes?

What do each of these root causes look like in tarot? Name one card for each and explain why you chose it.

1 | Moina feels certain that everyone will laugh at her writing. She can't face that humiliation.

  • Root Cause Card: _____

  • Why I Chose It: _____

  _____

  _____

  _____

2 | The story Moina wants to write is a thinly veiled autobiography. Moina's had a tough life, and she's nervous about reliving it.

  • Root Cause Card: _____

  • Why I Chose It: _____

  _____

  _____

3 | Moina is ambivalent about taking the time to do something as "frivolous" as writing. In her family, keeping a clean house and holding down a steady job are the most important things.

• Root Cause Card: _____

• Why I Chose It: _____

_____

_____

Assignment 5.4

Look Deep: What "Should" I Do?
(or, How Can I Improve This Situation?)

We now return to that thorny question: "What should I do?" The first time we had a crack at this question, we were reading for prediction (Look Far). We turned "What should I do?" into a more powerful question: "What is likely to happen if…?"

This time we're reading for insight (Look Deep), and once again we're going to slightly alter the question by taking back our power and removing the "should." Instead, we're going to ask, "What can I change about myself to improve this situation?" Or, more succinctly, "How can I improve this situation?" As we explore this question, we'll pay particular attention to any hopes and fears that color our view of the situation.

Instructions

1 | For each of these problems, I've highlighted one of the answers from Assignment 5.3. Look up the card you chose to describe that answer, and set that card aside.

2 | Now that you have the answer to what was going to happen, your client—Frieda, McGregor, or Moina—is asking "What should I do?" i.e., "What is likely to happen if I…" Imagine three possible answers—three different hypothetical paths the client might take. What cards might represent these three possible answers?

    For example: In the case of the first scenario, "Frieda's Heartache," we're going to pretend that the root cause is option two: Frieda and Harry have found they are at opposite ends of a seemingly unbridgeable political divide. Frieda asks you, "What should I do?" Your job is to come up with three possible approaches.

3 | Then, having decided what those possible paths are and which cards represent them, you're going to shuffle the deck and draw a card randomly. As in Assignment 5.2, this card will likely not be one of the three cards that you chose, and that is fine. If it is? Also fine.

Scenario 1: Frieda's Heartache

Relations are strained between Frieda and her grown son, Harry. He lives nearby, but they haven't talked in months. Frieda and Harry have opposing and firmly held political views.

They can't talk without getting in an argument. Each feels disrespected. Frieda asks, "What should I do?"

- What card did you choose to describe this scenario in Assignment 5.3? Find it and set it aside. _____

- Rephrase the "should" question: How can Frieda improve the situation?

    - New Question: _____

- Imagine three possible paths. What three cards represent these? (There is no need to remove the actual cards from your deck; this is an imaginative exercise.)

    - Path One: _____

    - Representing Card: _____

    - Path Two: _____

    - Representing Card: _____

    - Path Three: _____

    - Representing Card: _____

- Shuffle the deck, leaving your first card set aside. Randomly draw one card. What does it signify, and what's your advice to Frieda?

    - Random Card: _____

    - My Interpretation: _____

    _____

    _____

    _____

    _____

• Advice I'd Give Frieda: _____

_____

_____

_____

_____

Scenario 2: McGregor's Dream

McGregor is having a recurring dream. He is always trying to go somewhere, but something always prevents him—a monster, a wrong turn, he forgot his keys…When McGregor was young, he was a "good kid." If his parents told him not to do something, he wouldn't do it. Now his parents are not around, and he is starting to yearn for adventure. McGregor asks, "What should I do?"

- What card did you choose to describe this scenario in Assignment 5.3? Find it and set it aside. _____

- Rephrase the "should" question: How can McGregor improve the situation?

    - New Question: _____

- Imagine three possible paths. What three cards represent these? (There is no need to remove the actual cards from your deck; this is an imaginative exercise.)

    - Path One: _____

    - Representing Card: _____

    - Path Two: _____

    - Representing Card: _____

    - Path Three: _____

    - Representing Card: _____

• Shuffle the deck, leaving your first card set aside. Randomly draw one card. What does it signify, and what's your advice to McGregor?

    • Random Card: _____

    • My Interpretation: _____

    _____

    _____

    _____

    _____

    • Advice I'd Give McGregor: _____

    _____

    _____

    _____

    _____

Scenario 3: Moina's Novel

Moina wants to write a novel. Every time she sits down to write, though, she gets distracted, or discouraged, or thinks of something more important to do. Moina feels certain that everyone will laugh at her writing. She can't face that humiliation. Moina asks, "What should I do?"

• What card did you choose to describe this scenario in Assignment 5.3? Find it and set it aside. _____

• Rephrase the "should" question: How can Moina improve the situation?

    • New Question: _____

• Imagine three possible paths. What three cards represent these? (There is no need to remove the actual cards from your deck; this is an imaginative exercise.)

    • Path One: _____

    • Representing Card: _____

    • Path Two: _____

    • Representing Card: _____

    • Path Three: _____

    • Representing Card: _____

• Shuffle the deck, leaving your first card set aside. Randomly draw one card. What does it signify, and what's your advice to Moina?

    • Random Card: _____

    • My Interpretation: _____

    _____

    _____

    _____

    _____

    • Advice I'd Give Moina: _____

    _____

    _____

    _____

"Priming the Pump": What We Just Learned

Every tarot reader has had the experience of blanking out while staring at a card. *I have no idea what this means!* It's the thing that drives new readers crazy, and rightly so.

But the series of exercises I've given you in this chapter is the best antidote I know for "tarot brain freeze." By forcing ourselves to come up with hypothetical approaches, outcomes, and answers and then asking what that would look like in tarot, we're doing what I call "priming the pump." You're forcing your brain to think about imaginary circumstances and events and turn them into tarot.

In fact, you will find that any time you have a question that is difficult to answer, priming the pump will improve your likelihood of getting an answer that makes sense. Your readings will be stronger, clearer, faster. If you take a moment to imagine possible answers and the cards that might go with them before you even start drawing, you have a much better chance of understanding whatever card you get for even the most ridiculous questions.

I'll give you an example: When he was fourteen, my son, who is the least metaphysically inclined person in the world, was obsessed with football in general and the Packers in particular. One day before he was about to watch a Packers game, he was attempting to have a conversation about it with me, the least football-inclined person in the world. I thought to myself, *How can we make this conversation interesting for him* and *interesting for me?*

As is so often the case, I had a Rider-Waite-Smith deck nearby, so I said, "All right. Let's see who's going to win this game." My son, to his credit, went along with it. I asked myself how I would know if the Packers were going to win—priming the pump, you see.

"What do their jerseys look like?" I asked.

"They're green," said my son.

"Okay," I said. "Let's see if there are any green jerseys in this deck."

And, of course, I found one, on the 7 of Wands. I said, "All right. If we get the 7 of Wands, the Packers are going to win." I fanned out the deck for him, he pulled a card, and it was, in fact, the 7 of Wands. And the Packers won!

I didn't really know what would happen if we got any other card. I didn't think about what would happen if he'd gotten, say, one of the naked-people cards, or the Wheel of Fortune, which has no people on it at all. I don't know what I would have done if that had happened, and I don't *expect* that this exact thing will happen every time, or ever again. This exact thing also will likely never happen to you, but I am certain something like it will. My point is that tarot is weird and wonderful, and sometimes it just gives you a freebie like that.

Why does priming the pump work? Who can say! But if we imagine tarot as a relationship between friends (and why shouldn't we?), it's like friends signaling to each other that they're looking for answers. It's as if your friend tapped you on the shoulder and said, "Can I pick your brain about something?" Right away, you'd start thinking about ways you could help or ideas you could offer. For whatever reason, tarot acts *just like that.*

● ● ● ● ● ● ●

Chapter 5 Final Assignment

Prime the Pump

For most of this chapter, you've been devoting yourself to engaging with the problems of fictional characters. For your final assignment, we'll be bringing this technique to bear on the problems of the most important person in the room: *you!*

Instructions

1 | **Description.** Choose an issue or problem you may have in your life, whatever it may be: something that is important to you right now and that you don't know how to answer.

   • My Problem: _____

   _____

   _____

   _____

   _____

   _____

2 | **Prime the Pump.** Come up with five possible answers to the problem. Five may seem like a lot, but you can include some ridiculous options if you like. ("I will go for a ride on public transportation and see an advertisement or a book someone's reading and it

will give me a great idea!") Then you're going to name the cards that would represent each of those answers. That's the "priming the pump" part.

You can even choose one answer to be a wild card; i.e., "An answer I haven't thought of yet." If you do, you'll need to know what a "wild card" looks like to you in tarot language. Is it the Fool? The Ace of Wands? The 2 of Swords?

• Option One: _____

_____

_____

• Representing Card: _____

• Option Two: _____

_____

_____

• Representing Card: _____

• Option Three: _____

_____

_____

• Representing Card: _____

• Option Four: _____

_____

_____

• Representing Card: _____

• Option Five: _____

_____

_____

• Representing Card: _____

3 | **Final Draw.** Once you've come up with five possible answers and their corresponding cards, shuffle the cards back into the deck. Then draw just one card, randomly, for your final answer.

• Card I Drew: _____

• My Interpretation: _____

_____

_____

_____

_____

_____

How close was your actual answer to any of those five possible answers you came up with? Maybe it turned out to be one of them exactly; maybe it didn't. Whatever it is, you should now be able to get some kind of information about it and some kind of guidance.

six
DESIGN A SPREAD

What is a spread? Chances are, if you've looked through the Little White Book that came with your tarot deck, you've seen plenty of spreads—layouts that involve several cards at once. The most common one by far is the Celtic Cross, which uses ten cards to examine the before, the after, the whys and hows, the givens and potentials and challenges of any particular situation. The Celtic Cross is a powerful general spread, which is why it's so popular. But it can be overwhelming, too, especially if you dive right in the first week you've ever cracked the deck. You might end up trying to make so many connections that you end up with a rat's nest of threads, the gnarled mess of abstractions I call "fuzzy tarot." And when you have only one or two ideas about what each card might mean, putting even two cards together can cause you to short-circuit.

I always think of the great Divination Class scene from *Harry Potter and the Prisoner of Azkaban*, when Ron is trying to read his tea leaves: "Oh yeah...well, Harry's got a sort of wonky cross...that's trials and suffering. And, uh, that there could be the sun, and that's happiness, so...you're gonna suffer...but you're gonna be happy about it?"[11]

You might feel like you're lost before you even begin.

11 | *Harry Potter and the Prisoner of Azkaban*, directed by Alfonso Cuarón (Burbank, CA: Warner Bros., 2004).

Reading in Two and Three Dimensions

This is why we've spent so much time building up deeper relationships and wider connections with each card before venturing into spread design. We've also taken some time to figure out how to ask well-constructed, self-empowering questions. To tell the truth, I think you can get to the heart of most well-constructed questions quickly and effectively using only two- and three-card spreads. Really, that's all the Celtic Cross is: a collection of two- and three-card spreads that have all been merged together into one great ten-card beast. By deconstructing it, you can pick and choose what you need to know, in the order you need to know it.

In chapter 5, we learned to ask questions and find answers with a single card. In this chapter, we extend that skill into multi-card readings. We begin with two- and three-card spreads, and then at the end, we explore larger DIY spreads that can answer any genre or form of question.

If you can read a single card—which you've already proven you can do—you can read multiple cards. Spreads economize on time: rather than asking questions sequentially, you get to ask them kind of all at once and then pick your way through the information they offer up. You also get to look at the relationships between the cards and extract more meaning from them. How do you extract meaning from multiple cards? Well, by assigning each card a role to play. Spreads define the function of each card, which essentially gives the card an extra layer of meaning by restricting its sphere of influence.

If you ask a question and you draw a single card, that card could mean something that's going to happen, or something worth trying, or something to avoid—you can see right away how this kind of loose interpretation makes reading difficult. The same card could be advice ("Do this!"), or it could be a warning ("Don't do this!"). Honestly, it's a wonder anyone makes it more than a week reading tarot.

Much of the difficulty caused by loose interpretation can be solved simply by asking good questions, which we learned to do in the last chapter. We can solve even more by designing spreads. If you're not entirely sure when you look at a card whether it's something you're telling yourself or something you're afraid of, something you want or something you're projecting, give it a job. By assigning a role to the card, you're saying, "Okay, your job is to tell me what I fear." Or, "Your job is to tell me the inner reality." "Your job is to tell me what the advice is."

Each card can have a different, limited task. By narrowing down the interpretation so that the card can only speak in a particular way, you make it a little bit easier on yourself to find the meaning you want within the context you're working with. In my own practice, I actually use mostly two- and three-card spreads. Sometimes I'll do a five-card spread, which, conceptually, is almost always just a two-card reading and a three-card reading put together.

In this modular way, you can build quite complex structures out of very simple ones. I find it helpful to just start with two or three cards and then add more, following whatever it is the client wants to know more about. I'll never have more than ten to twelve cards out at a time. By layering the reading, you elicit the meaning bit by bit, meeting the question where it's at.

Cloud Computing, Tarot Style

People often say to me, "I know the meanings for each card, but I have trouble putting them together and reading a spread." This is completely understandable. If you've learned your meanings from a LWB, you've got a handful of abstract concepts. You rub them together like a couple of sticks, but they just won't ignite.

Let's suppose your friend has come to you asking for advice about the job they're applying for. You decide on a "Do/Don't" spread. You've drawn the 8 of Wands ("Do") and the High Priestess ("Don't"). The LWB that came in the box suggests the High Priestess means "mystery." It also says the 8 of Wands represents "activity." *Mystery, activity*, you think, staring out the window. Your friend looks at you expectantly, reaching for their tea. Your cat walks in and sits on the cards. *Activity, mystery…I got nothing.* Maybe you admit you don't get it. Or maybe you babble vaguely about how something is about to happen and it might be mysterious. Or maybe you say, "We need a clarifying card," or "Let's re-draw that, I wasn't concentrating."

Fortunately, this isn't going to happen to you, because you've been working your way through this book. You aren't relying on two or three abstract, inscrutable ideas about each card. You've been *living* with them. You know how they *feel*. A "diffuse cloud of cognition," a wealth of meaning, surrounds each card!

Great, you may be thinking. *Now you're saying my reading could mean virtually anything!* Ah, no, my friend. Let's have a look at those "diffuse clouds of cognition" again. You remember the High Priestess cloud from chapter 2? Let's do one for the 8 of Wands as well, and let's compare them.

Yes, there's a lot of information in these maps. There's even more in your mind. (And yes, "mystery" is in the High Priestess's realm, just as "activity" is in the 8 of Wands's.) But not all of this information is relevant or useful. Not all of it makes sense given the context. What you want are just the bits that matter.

You asked for information on "Do" and "Don't"—what's helpful and what's not helpful for your friend's situation. That means that when you look at the High Priestess and the 8 of Wands, you want to be thinking about the ways they're different, even opposite one another.

One thing I perceive right away is that the High Priestess is watery and the 8 of Wands is fiery. This is interesting to me, but I keep digging. The most striking opposite I encounter has something to do with secrets versus communication. The High Priestess is famously secretive and esoteric. You can't read that scroll she's got peeking out of her robes, and her mouth is closed. The 8 of Wands, by contrast, lets it all hang out. The 8 of Wands *thrives* on publicity, on viral tweets, on freedom of information.

Remember, your friend is asking for advice about the job they're applying for. So, given this spread and in this context, the High Priestess and the 8 of Wands could mean something like, "Do communicate. Don't be secret." And the way you would translate this for your friend might be something along the lines of: "You might want to do something to push your application along—make a phone call, check in, ask if there's anything else you can provide. If they ask you about that twelve-month gap in your resume, don't be secretive. Be upfront and tell them about the year you had to take off to take care of your mom. Maybe you thought that was too much information, but they will understand."

You may even recognize that in addition to being opposite in some respects, the High Priestess and 8 of Wands have something in common—something about travel, or maybe that weird thing about the "bow and arrow," which you think is interesting because it reminds you of the way your friend is aiming for the job. However, if that isn't relevant or useful, you don't feel obliged to mention it. My word clouds may or may not look like yours. That doesn't matter a bit. The point is, you actually know a ton about these cards, and if you give yourself a second to muse on them, what they're trying to say can and will come into focus.

Also, I should emphasize that it's not as if you have to sketch this out with literal word clouds, like some mad physicist, scrawling models of reality on a paper napkin. No! The human mind is a marvel of pattern recognition. In practice, it's going to be much more like you're holding the High Priestess and 8 of Wands in your mind, and you're sensing silence on the one side and chatter on the other.

It will happen seemingly instantaneously, because that's what the right brain is like. And once that happens, the only job left is to open your mouth and translate this thing you just grasped into English, in a way that is relevant and useful for the person sitting with you.

Chapter 6 Assignments: An Overview

In chapter 5, we learned to "prime the pump" and get results from single-card readings. In this chapter, we're going to have a close look at the theory and application of two-card spreads, and then we're going to have a close look at the theory and application of three-card spreads. You're going to be doing quite a few two- and three-card readings for hypothetical scenarios.

Then, you're going to use a spread-designing tool and come up with your own spreads to address a few more hypothetical scenarios. And finally, you're going to design your own all-purpose spread—the one you're going to pull out when someone asks you for a general reading.

By the time you finish chapter 6, you'll have done about a dozen proper readings—and don't try to tell me they're not legitimate just because they're mostly for fictional characters! Tarot doesn't care about that. By the end of this chapter, you should feel confident calling yourself a tarot reader. Don't let anybody tell you otherwise!

I recommend that you do no more than one or two of the readings at a time so that you can give each of them the best of your attention. Reading a lot of spreads in a row, especially if you're using the same deck for all of them, can exhaust your imagination until everything starts to look the same. That kind of interpretive burnout happens to all of us; it's normal. But the good news is that in twenty-four hours, you're bound to have a fresh brain that can make all kinds of brilliant, insightful new connections. And it's totally reasonable to just do one reading every day (or every other day) and take a few weeks to get through this chapter.

Two-Card Spreads: The Theory

Two-card spreads are excellent for all kinds of things: choices, decisions, relationships; any time a path forks; any time you have two things that are opposed to each other. Binaries, polarities, dichotomies, pairs—these are the stuff of two-card draws. Broadly speaking, I think there might be three general categories of two-card spreads: yes/no contrasts, inner/outer contrasts, and what I call two-of-a-kind.

Yes/No Contrasts

Yes/no contrasts help you isolate better and worse choices by assigning value: something you want more of in your life and something you want less of in your life. Some examples of these are:

- Strengths/weaknesses
- Advantages/drawbacks
- What nourishes you/what drains you
- Something to embrace/something to let go of
- Do/don't

There's something very clarifying about playing two cards off each other. For example, if I draw the 7 of Swords as "Do," it could mean anything from thinking outside of the box to stealing off in the night. But if I draw the 8 of Pentacles as "Don't" to the 7 of Swords' "Do," that throws their differences into relief and highlights something much more specific, perhaps something having to do with using my trickster skills rather than my worker bee skills.

Inner/Outer Contrasts

Inner/outer contrasts assume that there's something familiar, personal, and close to you as well as something that is farther, distant, and removed from you. Here, we're not assigning values as we are in the yes/no contrasts; one is not necessarily better than the other. They're just different. Here are a few examples:

- What my gut says/what I'm telling myself
- Inner reality/outer appearance
- Situation/conflict
- Self/other
- Known/unknown

One of the more interesting inner/outer contrasts I've used is "something to look for/ something to try." Something to look for is going to be handed to you in your environment; it's going to manifest in some way; it's predictive. Something to try is going to be something you're actually going to try and bring about; a way that you can act or a lesson you can embody. This can work particularly well as a Card of the Day practice.

Two-of-a-Kind Spreads

Most of the time when we're at a crossroads, it's not immediately obvious which is the right option; they seem equal. *Six of one, half dozen of the other*, we say to ourselves, scratching our heads.

Perhaps the most obvious two-of-a-kind spread is the relationship spread: Person A and Person B. It's perfect for anyone who wants to ask about their love life (unless "It's complicated"!). You can get so much information about the two people concerned just by looking at the way the figures in the cards are relating to each other. You could use their gaze: what or who they're looking at. You could see if they have basic compatibility: e.g., if they're both Wands cards, or if they're both majors, say. You could also use elemental theory (earth and water get along; earth and air clash), if you're into that.

The "Two of a Kind" spread I use perhaps the most often is: Option A/Option B. Any time you're faced with a binary choice or decision (*What if I make a move?/What if I hold off?* for example) you can ask tarot to give you some insight as to what you can expect if you follow one path or the other. The decision, of course, still remains yours. But forewarned is forearmed, as they say.

Card One	Card Two	Use
Inner	Outer	For example, the difference between appearance and reality, or the things we think versus the things we say
Something to look for	Something to try	This is a great pairing to try if you draw two Cards of the Day
Self (Person A)	Other (Person B)	This is great for inviting insights into any two-person relationship, romantic or otherwise
Situation	Conflict	A bit like the first two cards of the Celtic Cross: "what covers you" and "what crosses you"
What you're telling yourself	What your gut says	Good for sorting out projections from truth
Greatest fear	Greatest desire	Good for understanding motivations
Do	Don't	Self-explanatory
Advantage	Drawback	Self-explanatory
Strength	Weakness	Variation on do/don't; also: limits/superpowers
What you understand	What you don't understand	Good for figuring out where you need to shine more light
What nourishes you	What drains you	Good for pointing out helpful and unhelpful factors
Something to let go of	Something to embrace	Very good for suggesting concrete actions
Option A	Option B	Great for just gaming out two different paths

• • • • • •

Assignment 6.1
Two-Card Spreads

Binaries, contrasts, forks in the road, dialectics. Let's dive in!

Instructions

I've created a variety of sample readings about our friends from chapter 5 and some potential problems they might be facing. For each one, choose any two-card format you feel might draw out useful information, and see what kind of answers or advice you can give these characters. You'll want to write a few sentences interpreting each card, and a few more summing up what they seem to mean together.

Scenario 1

Moina has a story she is thinking of telling in front of an audience, but she's not quite sure. How can you help her?

• Two-Card Spread I Chose: _____

• Card One and My Interpretation: _____

_____

_____

• Card Two and My Interpretation: _____

_____

_____

• What These Cards Mean Together: _____

_____

_____

_____

Scenario 2

McGregor has a new boyfriend. He's excited, curious, and nervous. What can you tell him about his new relationship?

- Two-Card Spread I Chose: _____

- Card One and My Interpretation: _____

\
_____

_____

- Card Two and My Interpretation: _____

\
_____

_____

- What These Cards Mean Together: _____

\
_____

_____

_____

_____

Scenario 3

Pam is exhausted. There's just too much going on. Can you help her prioritize what's important?

- Two-Card Spread I Chose: _____

- Card One and My Interpretation: _____

\
_____

_____

• Card Two and My Interpretation: _____

_____

_____

• What These Cards Mean Together: _____

_____

_____

_____

* _____

Scenario 4

Aleister has a job interview tomorrow. Can you offer some advice about what to expect, or how he should present himself?

• Two-Card Spread I Chose: _____

• Card One and My Interpretation: _____

_____

_____

• Card Two and My Interpretation: _____

_____

_____

• What These Cards Mean Together: _____

_____

_____

_____

_____

Scenario 5

Choose a question of your own having to do with a choice, decision, or relationship. Pick a two-card spread to answer it, and then try the reading.

• Two-Card Spread I Chose: _____

• Card One and My Interpretation: _____

_____

_____

• Card Two and My Interpretation: _____

_____

_____

• What These Cards Mean Together: _____

_____

_____

_____

_____

Three-Card Spreads: The Theory

If two-card spreads are great for choices, contrasting things, and relationships, then three-card spreads provide what I call three-dimensional information. They provide depth. They're wonderful for getting at causes, motivations, and trajectories.

Trajectory Spreads

The most famous three-card reading—the one that everybody tries at some point—is the PPF: past, present, future. I think it works particularly well because the past and present are elements you already know, and that makes it easier to read the future; you can see a trajectory, recognize a story.

The window you use for past/present/future can be as broad or as narrow as you like. It could be the very recent past, like yesterday, and the very near future, like tomorrow. Or you could go as far back as a lifetime or a generation. It all depends on what you're comfortable reading and the nature of the question you're asking.

Other trajectory-based spreads are the "causes/current situation/outcome" spread and the "beginning/process/results" spread. Even though a lot of these spreads are similar, using different phrases helps pinpoint the exact nuance you want. As any pollster or statistician knows, the way you frame the question frames the answer. So, it's worth choosing your words carefully!

Two Cards, Plus

Many three-card spreads are simply enhanced two-card spreads. Often when we're looking at uncertain situations, we make the mistake of thinking there's only two possible realities involved: one is the reality that already exists, and one is the reality that potentially could. But a third element could be something you've not thought of, or something that's beneath the surface, or something that lies between or beyond them. Why dwell on your fears and hopes (a two-card spread) without also considering the reality (a three-card spread)? What's the point of knowing your obstacles and solutions (a two-card spread) without knowing your destination (a three-card spread) too?

Three-card spreads can be a roadmap to diversifying and broadening your options, but the one thing they invariably give you is perspective. I've provided a table of several useful three-card spreads, but it's only a starting point. Dream up your own!

Card One	Card Two	Card Three
Past	Present	Future
Causes	Current situation	Outcome
Subconscious	Conscious	Projections
Beginning	Process	Results
Obstacle	Goal	Help
Do	Middle road	Don't
What you understand	What you don't understand	What you need to know
Fears	Reality	Hopes
What you're leaving behind	What you'll find	What you seek
Your true feelings	Your mask	The difference (why they're not the same)
Something hidden	Something known	Something to consider

• • • • • •

Assignment 6.2

Three-Card Spreads

Causes, motives, trajectories, narratives. Let's take this into three dimensions!

Instructions

In this exercise, we're going to deal with situations from popular culture or fiction—partly because it's interesting, and partly to reinforce the point that stories are everywhere you look. Pick a three-card spread to answer each of these questions. Then draw the cards and try the readings. You'll want to write a few sentences interpreting each card, and a few more summing up what they seem to mean together.

Exercise 1

Choose a favorite song. Consider the point of view of the narrator singing the song. A majority of songs take place from a first-person narrator point of view, which helps you identify who's speaking and what their problem is. Even for the ones that are in second-person ("You Don't Own Me") or third-person ("She Drives Me Crazy"), you can still pick out a protagonist. You can choose a love song, a breakup song, an "I want" song, an "I'm the master of the universe" song, or a "The law is out to get me!" song—whatever you like.

Whatever kind of song you choose, figure out the problem and then choose a three-card spread to help the character in question gain some insight into what's going on with their problem. If they shoulda put a ring on it, and they didn't, what's the alternative? Where do we go from here?

- Three-Card Spread I Chose: _____

- Cards I Drew:

    1. _____

    2. _____

    3. _____

• My Interpretation of Each Card: _____

_____

_____

_____

_____

• What These Cards Mean Together: _____

_____

_____

Exercise 2

Choose a favorite story or a scene from a favorite story. It could be a book, a movie, or even a video game or graphic novel. Consider the protagonist's situation. (Chances are, the protagonist knows less than you do about what's going on in the larger plot.) Select a moment where the hero of the story has a dilemma or issue that they're trying to solve, and then choose a three-card spread for them and see what advice you can offer.

• Three-Card Spread I Chose: _____

• Cards I Drew:

    1. _____

    2. _____

    3. _____

• My Interpretation of Each Card: _____

_____

_____

_____

_____

• What These Cards Mean Together: _____

_____

_____

Exercise 3

Choose a question of your own that concerns a timeline or addresses causes, effects, and motivations, or where you as the protagonist must act with unknown information. Pick a three-card spread and try reading.

• Three-Card Spread I Chose: _____

• Cards I Drew:

1. _____

2. _____

3. _____

• My Interpretation of Each Card: _____

_____

_____

_____

_____

• What These Cards Mean Together: _____

_____

_____

Assignment 6.3
Design-Your-Own Spreads

Now that you have some practice working with two or three cards at a time, it's time to get creative and design your own spread—which is easier than you think.

What we're going to do here is work with a sizeable bank of possible positions or "labels" that can help you focus the information you're trying to evoke from the cards. You choose the positions you think will speak most directly to the scenarios I've given in each problem; you draw the cards; finally, you interpret the meanings.

I've sorted the labels into a few different categories, just to make things simpler: who, when, subject, influences, intentions. You can use *any* combination of these, and you don't have to hit every category. For example: Most likely, every spread you will ever read concerns a person, but that doesn't mean you have to have a "who" card. Every spread you will ever read is about some particular subject, but that doesn't mean you have to have a "subject" card. And if you don't see a label that works perfectly, *go ahead and make one up.*

I've provided three different but very typical questions that you can play with; all are based on questions I've received as a working tarot reader. You can design a spread of any kind that you like to try and answer them. As I've said, it's often a good idea to combine two- and three-card spreads to build larger spreads. So, for example, for a relationship spread you might use one position for Partner 1 and one position for Partner 2, and then you might add the past/present/future of the relationship to that, resulting in an easy five-card reading.

Or, for example, you could put together situation/conflict, which is essentially the center of the classic Celtic Cross spread, where they're called "what covers you" and "what crosses you." Then you could add fears/hope/reality to that, or causes/outcome. Whatever it is that rouses your curiosity when you read the question, that's a potential position. See what you can come up with. Spread design is a lot of fun!

One caveat: be sure you don't have too many synonyms within the spread. For example, if you're assigning one card to be "what to pursue" and a different card to be "what to embrace," you may find when you try to read them that they converge a little bit too much to be useful. The same issue might come up if you had both "what's blocking you" and "what to let go of." It's important to have different language choices, but beware of reading twice for what is essentially the same thing. You want the most economical but *informative* spread you can devise.

Instructions

1 | Read the question.

2 | Design a spread, using the tags provided (plus any others you want to add) to mark positions.

3 | Draw the cards and try the readings. You'll want to write a few sentences interpreting each card, and a few more summing up what they seem to mean together.

Who

you
your boss
your parent
your friend
your coworker
your partner
Partner 1
Partner 2
your mentors
your rival

When

now (present)
past
recent past
near future
future

Subject

love
health
finances
home
career
body
friendships
travel
mind
hobbies
spirit
life purpose

Influences

pros
cons
problem
situation
solution
what blocks you
what helps you
what traps you
what nourishes you
emerging influences
receding influences
messages
environment

Influences (cont.)

positive influences
negative influences
conscious thoughts
unconscious motives
attitudes
what you seek
inner reality
outer appearance
hopes
fears
causes
effects
meaning

Intentions

what to pursue
what to let go of
what to embrace
what to avoid
what you can't change
what you can change
what you need to know
what action to take
what to take from the past
what to find in the future

Scenario 1

William is in love with his best friend Luke's girlfriend, Maude. What can you tell him?

- Three-Card Spread Design:

[   ]   [   ]   [   ]
___   ___   ___

- Cards I Drew:

  1. _____

  2. _____

  3. _____

- My Interpretation of Each Card: _____

_____

_____

_____

_____

- What These Cards Mean Together: _____

_____

_____

Scenario 2

Greta and Frieda are thinking of starting a business, but they don't have funding and they're still in school. What's your advice?

- Three-Card Spread Design:

_____   _____   _____

- Cards I Drew:

1. _____

2. _____

3. _____

- My Interpretation of Each Card: _____

_____

_____

_____

_____

- What These Cards Mean Together: _____

_____

_____

Scenario 3

Sam lost his father, whom he was very close to, six months ago. He's having trouble concentrating and "moving on." How can you help?

- Three-Card Spread Design:

- Cards I Drew:

  1. _____

  2. _____

  3. _____

- My Interpretation of Each Card: _____

  _____

  _____

  _____

  _____

- What These Cards Mean Together: _____

  _____

  _____

Chapter 6 Final Assignment

Design Your Own All-Purpose Spread Using Five Cards or More

Now, at last—as you might have guessed—it's time to read for yourself. But although I know you're a very specific person with very specific questions, concerns, and needs, in this exercise you're going to come up with a general, all-purpose spread.

In your hopefully long career as a tarot reader, you are going to encounter the inevitable friend or client who says, "I don't know what I want to talk about in my reading," or, "I don't have any general ideas about what could be better or worse in my life," or, "Just tell me my future!" Now, I always feel rather skeptical when people tell me they have no idea what they want to read about. Who doesn't have problems?! Nevertheless, our aim as tarot readers is to help, so we need a spread that can provide some kind of insight, even if there is zero input from the person facing us.

Your general-purpose spread could be composed of subjects: home, partner, career, things like that. Or you could do something that looks at the person's life in a more holistic way, helping them figure out the type of energies and attitudes that will help them, and what no longer serves.

Instructions

1 | Come up with your own general, all-purpose five-card spread, using the tags listed in the last assignment as a starting point. You can certainly use more than five cards if you like.

2 | Once you're done designing the spread, take it for a spin. You can think of a situation of your own that you'd like a reading on, you can focus on a general area of your life, or you can leave it completely open. You can read for a good friend instead of yourself, if you like. It's just an opportunity to see how your spread works in practice.

3 | Document your results. You'll want to write a few sentences interpreting each card, and a few more summing up what they seem to mean together.

Note: With really general spreads, it can be particularly helpful to "prime the pump," as we learned to do in the last chapter. For example, you could say to yourself, *If this spread wants to give me advice about my upcoming move, I might see the Chariot or the Knight of Cups.*

seven

RITUALS, ETHOS, PRAXIS

Now that you have a working knowledge of your cards, it's time to take the show on the road and read for others. First, we take care of our spiritual hygiene: i.e., opening and closing rituals. We think about the practical limits of our art: *What can and can't I read for?* Then we think about the ethical limits of our skill: *What should and shouldn't I read for?* And we also engage in some good old-fashioned logistics, so you have what you need when you first step out the door as a tarot reader.

We'll start with the purely pragmatic concerns and work our way into the more metaphysical ones. The first couple of exercises simply address what you need to know ("Fortune-Telling Laws and Liabilities Research") and what you need to have ("The Packing List")—the legal structures and financial complications you may encounter, and what it's useful to have on hand in a reading setup. *Even if* you don't intend to go pro, you'll want to think about these considerations. They are bound to come up in conversation with friends and family, and if you don't know the answers, they just get in the way when you're trying to read.

The ethos assignments ("The Rules" and "The Spiel") build on what we began in chapter 4. In that chapter, we articulated some of our beliefs about the way tarot works. In this chapter, we face the test of our beliefs. If you believe that a benevolent spirit informs your readings, does that mean they can tell your client it's a good idea to quit that job? Have that surgery? Leave their relationship? How do you sort out your personal opinions from spiritual advice? What is the difference between empowering a client and controlling a client? Where do you draw the line?

185

Ritual Matters

Finally, we design a ritual praxis. Why does ritual matter? It matters because during the special interval when we read tarot, we're not really in a normal headspace. For most of our waking lives, we live in a world where cause and effect are straightforward. The ways in which we know things and find things out are predictable, and the idea that you can get insight and information in an uncanny way from outside is almost ludicrous! In order to read tarot at all, you have to put yourself in a particular mind frame, one that's distinct from your normal, everyday, shopping-for-cereal-in-Aisle-8-of-the-supermarket way of looking at the world.

The time we spend in that special headspace is the *oracular moment*, a term I originally got from the tarot reader and quantum physicist Yoav Ben-Dov. What's an oracular moment? Well, it has to do with the idea that at the moment of a reading, we access something beyond ourselves; something bigger than ourselves. We get a glimpse of our connection to the larger pattern and our ability to perceive and work with that.

How you think this works is up to you; it's different for everyone. And really, you don't have to have a mechanistic theory of why divination works. (Auras? Rays? Psychic brainwaves?!) In fact, personally, I think those kinds of material theories may just get in the way. But I do think it helps to have a working metaphorical model for what's going on in the oracular moment.

I like to think that when we divine, we enter a kind of backstage behind reality. Real life is what plays out in front of the curtain; backstage is where we have the props and the winches, the hoists and the lights—everything that makes the reality appear like reality. When we go "backstage" in a reading, we're finding out how things work; why things look the way they look; why *this* is cast in shadow and *that* shows up in the light. And that's very useful information.

In our normal, mundane reality, information is a little harder to come by. If we take that mundane-reality frame of mind into a reading, we handicap ourselves with doubt. We find ourselves limiting what we think we can know to our five senses.

Of course, it's possible to go overboard in the other direction. It's possible to convince yourself that *everything* is a relevant sign and an urgent oracle, and before you know it you're in pins-and-red-string territory. If every time you walk across the street and a pebble drops you take it as a sign of something requiring your attention, you're likely to drive yourself crazy. There's only so much we can take in our relationship to the field of meaning.

So for the purposes of remaining grounded, sane tarot readers, let's just say it's *only* when we do a tarot reading that we open ourselves up to the larger patterns and meanings all around us. After that we shut ourselves down again, so we can live like normal human beings.

How do we open up that space? Well, that's going to be up to you. In the final assignment in this chapter, you'll be figuring out which rituals work for you.

. . . . . .

Assignment 7.1

Fortune-Telling Laws and Liabilities Research

Reading tarot for anyone other than yourself is, according to the eyes of the law, "fortune-telling." Fortune-telling exists in a legally liminal space that varies greatly depending on what country, province, state, or county you live in; enforcement is also widely variable. Know your liability so you can minimize unexpected and unwelcome threats to your practice.

Local Laws

You'd be surprised—lots of places (at least in the United States, which is where I live and the place I know best) have official bylaws on "fortune-telling," which can involve astrology, palmistry, tarot, or other practices. Some have outright bans; others impose penalties or fees or licensing requirements.

In practice, many of these are never enforced. A great many are just old-time statutes most have forgotten about and everyone ignores, like Boston's law against eating peanuts in church or Fargo's law against dancing with a hat on.[12] When fortune-telling laws do get challenged, it generally turns out that our national regard for free speech takes hold and the fortune teller is protected under the First Amendment.[13]

In 2015, the Supreme Court issued a decision in Reed v. Town of Gilbert that concerned something known as the "content discrimination principle."[14] Basically, it determined that, within reasonable limits, you can't ban signage based on whether you approve or disapprove of the content in the sign. This makes it legal for fortune tellers to literally hang out their shingle. The state can, though, license and regulate fortune tellers based on what's known as "professional speech doctrine" (Moore-King v. County of Chesterfield).[15] In many states (including my own), individual towns issue fortune-teller licenses for a nominal fee, and it wouldn't hurt you to get one if you plan on charging for tarot readings.

12 | For an example of some fascinating historical context, check out Christine Corcos, "Seeing It Coming since 1945: State Bans and Regulations of Crafty Sciences Speech and Activity," *Journal Articles* 37, no. 1 (Fall 2014): 39–114, https://digitalcommons.law.lsu.edu/faculty_scholarship/400/.

13 | Nick Nefedro v. Montgomery County, Maryland, et al., 414 Md. 585, 966 A.2d 850 (2010), https://casetext.com/case/nefedro-v-montgomery-county; Spiritual Psychic Science Church v. City of Azusa, 39 Cal. 3d 501, 217 Cal. Rptr. 225, 703 P.2d 1119 (1985), https://casetext.com/case/spiritual-psychic-science-church-v-city-of-azusa.

14 | Reed et al. v. Town of Gilbert, Arizona, et al., 576 U.S. 155 (2015).

15 | Moore-King v. Cnty. of Chesterfield, Virginia, 819 F. Supp. 2d 604 (2011), https://casetext.com/case/moore-king-v-county-of-chesterfield.

Maybe you don't consider your tarot practice "fortune-telling"; maybe you don't even consider it the least bit predictive. But as long as you earn any kind of income from reading cards, it's good to know the legal status of fortune tellers in your locality. It's also a good idea to include the line "for entertainment purposes only" on any of your promotional or merchandising materials.

Payment Processors

Local laws may be something of a joke when it comes to divination; they are more likely a reflection of local cultural biases than any kind of real threat for diviners. But in terms of payment, you may run into some serious real-life issues if you're dealing with any kind of payment that's not cold, hard cash. Many mainstream financial institutions consider fortune-telling a "high-risk business," and therefore have outright bans on processing payments for fortune-telling services.

For example, the education platform Teachable and the website builder Squarespace both currently process credit card payments through the payment processor Stripe. At the moment, Stripe *does not* allow any fortune tellers to use its services (although you won't find language specific to this in its fine print), so you are likely to lose your account sooner or later if you rely on them. There's a similar issue with SumUp and iZettle. This has happened both to me and to others I know. Fortunately, most platforms allow more than one payment processor. As of this writing, Square (which restricts "occult materials"), PayPal, and ApplePay are still safe choices for tarot services.

Should you end up banned by all the most familiar payment processors, there are a number of options that cater to "high-risk businesses," like PaymentCloud, Host Merchant Services, Durango, and Soar. They will charge you a premium, though.

Instructions

Research the following two questions and find out how they apply to you. File the info somewhere you can find it in the future and update as needed.

1 | What are the laws, statutes, ordinances, or bylaws governing fortune-telling in your country, state, county, or town? Are they enforced? Is a license available?

2 | Look into payment options (if you're reading professionally). If you accept payments through your website or directly, what payment processor do you use? Is fortune-telling among the processor's "restricted businesses"?

Assignment 7.2

The Packing List

If you're reading cards anywhere other than at your house, chances are you're going to pack up some tarot-related paraphernalia when you walk out the door. I don't know about you, but no matter where I'm going, I always forget something—I honestly have trouble remembering more than three things if I don't have a list.

What should you bring? There's a whole universe of tarot-adjacent accessories to consider: spread cloths, candles, incense, crystals, pendulum, runes…and don't forget tissues! Tissues are very important if you're a tarot reader. Things get emotional quickly, and you never know who'll need them.

Instructions

This is a short series of questions to help you sort out what you want to bring (and what you want to leave behind) when you're going out in the world to do readings. Make a list of which items from each category you want. File the list somewhere you can find it in the future and update as necessary.

1 | **Decks:** What decks will you bring? What are your current best decks for reading for others? Do you want to include any oracle decks, in addition to your tarot deck(s)?

2 | **Other Divinatory Tools:** Which ones will you bring? Pendulum? Runes? Bones?

3 | **Accessories:** Spread cloth? Crystals? Candles? Oils? Timer? Incense? Tissues?

4 | **Marketing:** Business cards? Any other product you might want to sell or show-and-tell?

_____

_____

_____

_____

_____

Assignment 7.3

The Rules

This exercise is intended to help you pinpoint your views on several common issues that come up when you read cards for other people. It's a framework for working out for yourself what your limits are as a reader. As you develop in your practice, your answers may change. Still, it's good to have a starting point, and to have an answer ready when someone asks.

The questions are very simple to ask, but maybe not so simple to answer. I've brought up every common controversy I know of in tarot—the ones people will ask you about, but also the ones you think about privately and may not be sure how you feel about.

After you've come up with your answers, it's a good idea to revisit these questions from time to time. For example, right now you may not feel like doing very much prediction; you may prefer to Look Deep than to Look Far. That may change over time. Or maybe you feel confident about timing, but then, after some months of practice and results, you find your timing predictions aren't working very well. So you back off from that a little bit. Or maybe you're fine with reading for "people who aren't in the room" (third parties), but then you get a client whose only desire is to spy on and gossip about everyone they know. So you change your policy about that.

These are not necessarily things that you have to talk to your client about (or anyone else, really), but they're good for you to know yourself. Have a position, and then later on you can change it if you need to.

Instructions

This is a series of topics you'll be asked about, sooner or later, if you read regularly. Take a moment to articulate your position on each one, recognizing that it's okay for your thoughts to evolve as you gain more experience as a reader. Note your answers on the following pages or, if you prefer, create a digital record you can refer to and update in the future.

1 | **Prediction:** Do you predict? How much free will do you think your client has? How far out do your predictions go?

2 | **Hypotheticals:** Do you feel comfortable reading about the future? ("If I do X, what will happen?") Do you feel comfortable reading for extended hypotheticals? ("Suppose I do X, and Y happens. What if I then do A? Or B?")

3 | **Projection:** How do you distinguish between your personal opinion and what the cards are saying? What is the difference in your mind, body, or attitude when expressing those two different perspectives? When you catch yourself expressing your own opinions, how do you convey that to the client? (Sometimes I'll just go ahead and say, "This is me speaking as a person / mom / woman, not as a tarot reader.")

4 | **Timing:** Do you have a system for judging when an event will take place? If so, what is it? Some readers use correspondences (Wands = soon, Pentacles = a long time from now, 6 of Swords = second decan of Aquarius = first week of February). Some use cards to show "signposts," events that might happen before or after the event, without any specific calendar information associated with them. Some don't answer timing questions at all.

5 | **Location:** Do you locate lost objects? If so, what's your method?

6 | **Third Parties:** Some readers won't read for the motives of those not in the room; some say they can't, and some say they won't. Personally, I will read the relationship between the client and the third party, one card for each. What's your policy?

7 | **Health Concerns:** What kind of questions do you feel comfortable answering about medical issues? What is your disclaimer? (I strongly recommend you always first suggest the client see a doctor.)

8 | **Is That Legal?** What will you do when you suspect a crime? Domestic abuse? A treatable addiction? What crosses a line for you and determines you must contact the police? What phone numbers, websites, or email contacts do you have on hand to offer support or services that go beyond what you do?

9 | **Big Questions of Fate:** How will you reframe the following questions: "Will I become rich / poor?" "Will I ever meet someone?" "Will I stay in this job forever?" "When will I die?"

10 | **Sacred Cards:** How do you feel about clients touching your cards? Is that okay? If not, how do you convey that to them without offending them?

11 | **Accuracy:** How do you indicate your degree of accuracy / certainty? (Some possible answers: "Eighty percent of the time, it turns out I'm accurate." "People tell me X happened just like I predicted.") Sometimes, you're not going to feel confident about a spread or interpretation, which is human, and it's best to be honest about that. What will you say when you are not sure about what you're reading? ("Who knows? We can try this technique. No guarantees." "Does that resonate? What would make more sense to you?" "I could be wrong! I just read the cards.")

12 | **Psychic:** It's a guarantee that someone will ask you if you're psychic or not. How do you understand the term *psychic*? Do you think you are, or not?

———

1 | **Prediction:** _____

_____

_____

2 | **Hypotheticals:** _____

_____

_____

3 | **Projection:** _____

_____

_____

4 | **Timing:** _____

_____

_____

5 | **Location:** _____

_____

_____

6 | **Third Parties:** _____

_____

_____

7 | Health Concerns: _____

_____

_____

8 | Is That Legal? _____

_____

_____

9 | Big Questions of Fate: _____

_____

_____

10 | Sacred Cards: _____

_____

_____

11 | Accuracy: _____

_____

_____

12 | Psychic: _____

_____

_____

• • • • • •

Assignment 7.4

The Spiel

If you read for people other than yourself, chances are the person across from you may not know much about tarot. They might have gone to a tarot reader a few times, or never; they're curious, or have tried it for themselves and now need somebody else to help them take the next step. A few introductory words go a long way toward setting people at ease.

This assignment is intended to help you introduce yourself and your tarot practice to the client. These are the questions I hear most often from those who are new to tarot, and which I've found most effective to address upfront. If you have an easy answer for each of them, you'll save yourself a lot of time and effort. Save your brain cells for reading tarot!

Personally, I love answering those "everything you ever wanted to know about tarot but were afraid to ask" questions from clients. Tarot is so different from anything most folks encounter in their everyday lives, and it's entirely understandable they want to know more. But at the same time, they're probably on the clock, they probably have pressing personal questions, and you don't want to waste their time.

So while they're getting comfortable, explain what you do and directly confront some questions they may have about tarot. You should be able to address all the issues in this assignment in a couple minutes, and then they'll be ready to dive into the reading with you.

I usually start the session with one question of my own: "Have you ever had a tarot reading before?" This establishes an important dynamic—that the reading is about the client, not about me. And it also allows me to adjust the spiel to their level of familiarity.

Instructions

1 | Each of the following questions address one thing your client will likely be curious about. Jot down your answers to each, and see if you can condense your answers into a single sentence. Your spiel should take you just a few minutes to get through. Note your answers on the following pages or, if you prefer, create a digital record you can refer to and update in the future.

   • **Who Am I?** In one sentence or two, what does the client need to know about you? You may want to share how long you've been reading and/or why you read tarot ("I help people solve problems and face uncertainties in their lives," for example). This is also a good opportunity to explain whether you are or aren't "psychic" and what that means, in case your client has preconceptions about that. (Only necessary in situations where you're reading for complete strangers.)

- **What Is Tarot?** Provide your best short, simple definition of what tarot is. ("Tarot is a way of expressing what's going on in your life in pictures," for example.)

- **"Do You Have a Question?"** How much info do you want from the client before you begin? Do you want very specific questions? Areas of concern? Nothing at all? Tell the client what works best for you. If the client isn't sure what they want, you can offer some examples of questions or subjects others have read about.

- **Fate? Or Free Will?** Briefly explain to the client how you use tarot to deal with the future. ("I believe we all choose our own fates, but tarot can show the direction we're currently headed," for example.)

- **Hard Cards:** Particularly if a client is new to tarot or nervous, it's a good idea to talk to them upfront about any cards that may frighten them, like Death, the Devil, or the 10 of Swords. What will you say?

- **Procedures:** If you have any expectations of your client, what are they? (Can they touch the cards? Shuffle with you? Is your reading a conversation or a monologue? Should they let you know if something doesn't make sense?)

2 | Practice your spiel with a friend (or just say it to the mirror, or your cat!) until you can deliver it in just a couple minutes. (Optional!)

———

- **Who Am I?** _____

_____

- **What Is Tarot?** _____

_____

- **"Do You Have a Question?"** _____

_____

• Fate? Or Free Will? _____

_____

• Hard Cards: _____

_____

• Procedures: _____

_____

_____

_____

_____

_____

_____

Chapter 7 Final Assignment

Opening and Closing Rites

Ritual is a signal to your spiritual self when you're open for business and when you're closed for business. You don't have to go over the top with this; you don't have to wear robes and a mask made of feathers or carry a rattle and sacrifice an animal. You can just light a candle and then blow it out afterward, if you like to keep things simple. Some folks need more to get themselves in the right headspace; you could use incense, lighting, crystals, perfumes, spread cloths—whatever it is that you noted in your Packing List.

Even more important than the trappings of ritual are the intentions that go with it. Because words carry intentions, I recommend you come up with something to say at the beginning and something to say at the end of your session—a few opening and closing words that convey your intent. You don't even have to believe what you're saying with all your heart in the moment you're saying it; the fact that you're saying the words counts for something: it inscribes your intention on the atmosphere around you and declares you to be a creature of will.

Opening Rituals

These are the elements that typically go into an opening ritual.

Banishing

You may be thinking, *Why (and what?!) do I need to "banish" before I've even sat down to read?* The theory is that you want to start in a spiritually cleansed, protected space before you step outside of normal reality. You may think the room you're in is clean and empty of spiritual influences, but if you had an argument with your partner in there this morning, or if you wrote an angry tweet? It's not. By "banishing," you assert that the space is now free of negative influences, and then you do your reading.

Magicians in the Golden Dawn tradition will do a Lesser Banishing Ritual of the Penta-gram, which you can look up anywhere. Those in Wiccan and Neopagan traditions often call the quarters. These different sets of rituals all have something in common: you are essentially calling upon each of the four directions (sometimes characterized as guardians, watchtowers, elements, or angels) for power and protection. This is the same as casting a circle.

Self-Empowerment

Often immediately following the banishing/quarter-calling (or integrated into it) is a state-ment of the magician's own power and central place. In the Lesser Banishing Ritual of the Pentagram, it's the Qabalistic cross. Having established a circle by calling on its four cardinal points, you establish yourself at the point in the center. You may add in references to up and down, or above and below, as in the Emerald Tablet of Hermes Trismegistus. It's a way of saying, "Here I am. I am a microcosm of the Universe, complete in myself. Because I know where and what I am, I am capable of doing a magical act or receiving special information."

Invocation

Having cleared the space and established protection on all sides, you get to call in your helpers, gods, and guides in whatever way you wish. You can use hymns of praise; you can read poetry of your own or others'; you can chant; you can speak extemporaneously. You can visualize white light and breathe in incense.

Dismissal (What to Do When You're Done)

When you're done, you move out of that space—not physically, but mentally, emotionally, and spiritually. Perhaps you blow out a candle and say, "The work is done." Perhaps you dis-miss your guides and spirits. Perhaps you put away your cards and crystals in a particular way or do something else to mark the end of the session. For example, when I do ancestor work, I say, "Depart in peace, and may we know one another from a distance." I want them looking out for me, but not breathing down my neck! When I'm doing readings, I personally use the Tree of Life, which is the Kabbalistic diagram of the ten sephiroth. I go up the Tree of Life before I begin, and I go down the Tree of Life when I return.

Dismissal, however simply you do it, is crucial. You know what's a great way to find out for yourself if tarot is "real," if you're still feeling skeptical this far into your studies? Try doing readings for three hours straight one afternoon. When you're done, skip the dismissal and see how you feel. You won't like it! You'll just want to go to bed or you'll sit staring into space and petting the cat. You'll be more tired than you should be after an afternoon of just talking to people. That's an aftereffect of having opened yourself up wider than you normally do; when you're reading tarot, you're allowing a whole lot of other people's stuff to pour through you.

Instructions

1 | Write and memorize your own quarter-calling or banishing rite. This is a method of locating yourself within the four directions (east, south, west, north) and between Heaven and Earth. It's a way of saying "I am here, and I am connected to the world around me." It's a way of calling on your guides to protect you while you work, and to clear out any unwanted influences. It can be as complex as the Golden Dawn's Lesser Banishing Ritual of the Pentagram, or as simple as lighting a candle and saluting each of the directions. Ideally, you'll want elements of banishing, self-empowerment, and invocation. Here are some resources you may wish to consult:

   • Assignment 2.3: 4 Suits Backwards: Elements

   • Assignment 4.4: Who You Gonna Call?

   • Chapter 8 in *Six Ways: Approaches & Entries for Practical Magic* by Aidan Wachter [16]

---

16 | Online resources for this abound and are constantly changing. Two good sources at the time of this writing are http://www.witchipedia.com/book-of-shadows/spells/calling-quarters and http://www.egreenway.com/wands8/envoke1.htm.

2 | Write and memorize your own dismissal rite, to be performed after drawing your cards or doing your magic. (You can write it below or, if you prefer, create a digital file you can refer to and update in the future.) When you're done with spiritual work, it's important to signal that you are grounding yourself and returning to ordinary reality. This can be as elaborate as walking backward around your circle, dismissing each direction, or as simple as snuffing out a candle. You can banish with laughter, ring a bell, clap your hands, eat something, or literally touch the ground with your hand. (I mentally climb down the Tree of Life.)

_____

_____

_____

_____

_____

_____

_____

_____

_____

eight
TAROT MAGIC

Friends, you are amazing. You've made it to the final chapter of this book. Congratulations! If you've gotten this far, you've done an immense amount of work and come a long way in your tarot practice, and I salute you—you have way more commitment and dedication than I had in my first year of learning tarot. I hope tarot is bringing you the fulfillment and enchantment you hoped it would, and I promise you that will only grow if you keep up the practice. Chapter 8 may be the end of the work you've done with this book, but it's only the beginning of a great adventure.

In our work up to this point, we've learned to do what tarot readers do: use the cards to gain information; that's divination. Now it's time to act on it; that's magic. Once you speak the language of tarot, you can use it not just to have conversations and learn the news—now you can argue back. You can persuade, negotiate, and compel. In this chapter, we'll explore several powerful spells to help you do just that.

In chapter 7 (and in my book *Tarot Correspondences*), I introduced the idea of "going backstage." We've contrasted the mindset of the ordinary world with the mindset we're in when we read tarot, and we've conjectured that being in a tarot mindset is like visiting the "backstage of reality." In divination, we take a step behind the curtain of reality and we get information—special information that is not normally accessible to us.

"BACKSTAGE"

THE READING		THE WORKING
THE DIVINER'S WAY	PERCEPTION	INTENTION	THE MAGICIAN WAY
	ACCEPTANCE & PERSPECTIVE	ACTION	

ORDINARY REALITY

Magic, by contrast, is the act of going backstage and changing things. When we change things backstage—whether it's the lighting, or the backdrop, or the costume our actors wear—we affect what happens in front of the curtain: i.e., reality as we perceive it.

Magical theory varies with every practitioner (and to some extent I think it *has* to be subjective, since every person's experience of magic is unique to them). But one of my own beliefs is that we're actually engaged in low-level, ambient magic all the time, though perhaps some of us do it with more intent and deliberateness than others.

Every time you psych yourself up to do something? That's an act of magic. Every time you tell yourself you're not good enough to do something? That's an act of magic. When you put on your makeup or cologne and set out to seduce someone? When you triple-check the cover letter on that job application and send it at 8:00 a.m. on Thursday because you heard that's when your prospective boss reads email? When you root for your favorite hockey team? When you pray to your God to heal a sick relative? Magic, all of it.

You may be thinking, *Well, then it sounds like magic is just psychology, or maybe religion.* And my answer to that is, I guess it depends what you mean by psychology or religion. Let's not worry about that right now. Let's just assume that you're capable of changing a great deal more in your life than you currently believe. And while we could argue any kind of change you intentionally affect in the world has an element of magic, there's a difference when you work within one of the traditional magical systems. In these systems, we work with symbol and concrete metaphor rather than expecting all the work to take place in our heads. In fact, I think that lends a certain humility to magic. It says, *I'm not necessarily doing this all by myself!*

The ultimate symbol system, perhaps, is language, and all along we've been talking about tarot as a language you can *get better at.* At this point, you've gone beyond "Do you speak English?" and "What time does the train leave?" It's time to learn those higher-order language skills: Negotiating deals! Flirting! Wrangling customer service! In life, we get what we want by saying just the right words at the right time to the right person—and tarot is like that. Now that you speak tarot, you get to call the shots. You get to make the choices, and you get to make things happen in your life. Like all symbol systems, the language of tarot interfaces with reality in ways that are subtle, profound, and will eventually change your life.[17]

Results, Differences, Offerings

"Within results are differences. Differences are offerings. And offerings are results."

On a summer morning in 2018, I woke up with these cryptic phrases echoing through my brain as I washed up on the shallow shores of consciousness. They were so weird and striking that as I drifted up to consciousness, I held very still for a minute to try and capture them and bring them back to the waking world. At first I was bewildered. *What could that mean?* But the more I thought about it, the more it seemed to me that these three phrases were a commentary on the relationship of divination and magic. Here's how I broke it down.

Within Results Are Differences

"Results" = the cards you draw in a tarot reading. You've asked a question, you've shuffled, you've drawn, you've gotten some results, and now you're interpreting them. But there's lots and lots of different meanings within each card—those are the "differences." It's up to each of us to sift through those infinite possible meanings as we hunt for the right interpretation.

Differences Are Offerings

As I consider those many meanings or "differences," I notice some of them are meanings that I would like the card to have. And some of them are meanings that I would prefer the card not to have. When I'm doing tarot magic, I get to choose which meanings I would like to have traction and significance in my life—that's my offering.

For example, some of the meanings of the 5 of Wands might be: conflict, strife, debate, sports, competitions…all of these possible meanings are the card's differences. I consider these

---

17 | In my book *Tarot Correspondences: Ancient Secrets for Everyday Readers*, there's also a fairly extensive section on tarot magic. A small fraction of the material in this module overlaps with that, and you may well find it useful to have the book on hand as a reference, especially for the Tree of Life spell. You can absolutely look up correspondences online instead of buying my book. But it's available and will save you some trouble, if that's useful to you.

differences, and I say, "You know what? Today, I would like the 5 of Wands to mean 'competition.' It's game night, and I am in the mood for a dose of healthy competition, and I don't really want the 5 of Wands to mean strife, because I'm not interested in dealing with interpersonal drama. I want this to manifest in a positive way; a spirit of healthy competition." My interpretation = my offering.

Offerings Are Results

This statement closes the loop. Before, "results" meant the cards I drew. Now, "results" means the reality I am living. It means my offerings—my interpretation of what the cards mean—are now the same as my lived reality. In other words, I've taken circumstances brought to me by chance (the cards I drew) and my own intentions (the way I interpret the cards) and blurred the difference between them. Now my intentions are fused with the forces of fate. Another way of putting it: even though I have no control over fate, I can hope to bring my thoughts and actions into closer alignment with what is to come. That's my theory—every act of interpretation involves this cycle. It's a feedback loop between reality and magical intent.

There are two ways of defining the verb "mean": to signify (i.e., "What does this symbol mean?") or to intend (i.e., "What do you mean to do?"). By interpreting cards, we decide what they signify—that's working with the first definition. By acting magically, we intend to create an effect—that's working with the second definition. Each of the exercises in this chapter encourages you to work with magical intent: not just to interpret, as we have till now, but to *act*.

Chapter 8 Assignments: An Overview

The exercises that follow are more like prompts than assignments. Take your time, do your best, make it special—because, as with all magic, what you get out of it is in proportion to what you put into it.

The first three assignments are spells. The word "spell" comes to us from Old English *spellian*, meaning "to tell" or "to speak," which is one more clue that human speech—our words, our utterances, our Logos—is inherently magical.[18] With these three assignments, you'll be

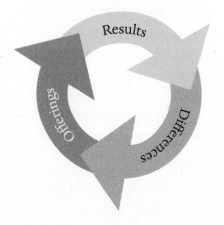

---

18 | Online Etymology Dictionary, s.v. "spell (v. 1)," updated February 27, 2022, https://www.etymonline.com/word/spell.

creating short but powerful speech-acts intended to bend the reality around you into a shape that is more to your liking.

The fourth assignment is also a spell, but a special one, intended to *un*-bend reality; i.e., to free yourself from the accumulated effects of a lifetime of unintentional ambient magic.

The next-to-last and the last assignment may include spells, but they are more properly described as workings—magical operations you yourself will compose, execute, and benefit from. They are creative acts that begin with tarot, but certainly don't end there—you can expect their effects to ripple subtly into your life in ways that you yourself will see and appreciate (whether or not anyone else does).

These are relatively freeform exercises, and we haven't included blank lines for you to fill in. You can document your magical efforts in any way you like—on your laptop, in a journal, in the blank pages at the end of this book. But *do* make some kind of record; that's a signal to your magical self that what you do matters and is worth preserving in the book that is your life. In ten years when you look back at this time, you want to be able to see the meaning, beauty, and significance of the investment that you made. If you do, I guarantee you will be able to say, in retrospect, "This changed my life."

Assignment 8.1

Card of the Day Spell

Now that you speak fluent tarot, it's time to use your new language to make magic! That's right—it's time to act in ways that change future outcomes! It's time to mildly alter the shape of reality!

The Card of the Day spell, which I introduced to the Fortune's Wheelhouse Academy Facebook group in 2018, has become a core practice for a lot of readers. It's incredibly simple, but incredibly powerful. And all it is, essentially, is a little poem based on your card draw.

Drawing a card is a lot like life. There's things you can't control: for example, the card you draw is random, and if you're a true tarot reader you accept it no matter what it is. But then there are things you can control: what the card means is up to you. The cards talk to you—but the spell lets you talk back. The cards say, "Here's how things are." The spell says, "I'd like to negotiate!" And there is always room for negotiation. "Spell" is related to the word "spiel"—it has to do with speaking. Of all of the meanings your card could represent, you're going to choose what you most want—the meaning you would like to bring forward into your day—and you're going to speak it into existence.

You can use keywords you've developed, or correspondences you look up, as a word bank. It can rhyme, or not. Your spell can be just one or two lines, or it can be more if you feel like it. Couplets work. Haiku works. I do, though, recommend that you keep your spell short so that you can memorize it. That way, at different points during the day, you'll be able to refer to it without having to look it up. When things are not going quite the way you wanted, you can tweak the spell if need be. Or you can recite it emphatically, in an effort to change the trajectory of the day. You can do whatever you want with the spell! It is your creation! And then, at the end of the day, you get to see how it worked out.

Even on days you draw the Tower, or the 10 of Swords, or both (which has happened to me), you get to choose what you make of them. A symbol gains its power from perception, and perception is driven by intent, and your intent belongs to you and you alone. Write a spell in the morning, and it will act as a compass, a shield, and a map for you for the whole day. If things are starting to go sideways, you can recite the spell (you can even modify it) and see if things get better.

Instructions

Now, how do you go about creating this powerful talisman?

1 | **Choose a format.** You can do couplets, haiku, rhymed, unrhymed, proverbs, mottos…
It doesn't really matter, as long as it's long enough to evoke a picture and short enough
to kind of remember. I like to do two-line spells, personally.

2 | **Write it in the present.** As with all magic, it's best to phrase your intention in the pres-
ent tense rather than the future, to make the outcome more real. (If I say "I will plant a
garden," that means the garden planting is taking place in the future, not now…and at
the end of the day, that will still be true.) There are even some who argue your magical
writings should be phrased in the past, as already accomplished.

3 | **Keep it concrete.** If you use abstract ideas (manifestation, transformation, balance),
you'll get a pretty vague sort of spell. Our magical selves work in metaphors. I've found
very concrete spells that appeal to the senses work well. They're open to interpretation
and hard to forget.

Chances are there are symbols in the card you can use as building blocks. But you
can use tarot correspondences—elements, astrology, numbers, Kabbalah, music, gem-
stones, whatever you like—to come up with the keywords.

For example, the Empress is associated with earth, Venus, roses, bees, sparrows, cop-
per, green, pink, swans, clovers, the night, vanilla, strawberries, sandalwood, roses, the
number three, and doors. So if I were to draw her card, I might write something like:

> *The sparrow flies through doors of night.*
> *Soft her wing and sure her flight.*

You now carry this image of ease and sweetness in your mind, ready to pour its
grace into your work, your love life, and any other journeys of mind or body that you
take today.

Even if you get a card that's a lot tougher to work with than the Empress—say, the
10 of Swords—you still get to put a word in with Fate about how you want it to show
up in your life. Here's one I wrote for the 10 of Swords a while back:

> *In the last days of the Twins,*
> *One story ends, and one begins.*

Just as good—or even better!—are your personal correspondences. If you notice on days you've drawn the 8 of Cups that you often dream of the ocean, use that. If you notice on days you've drawn the 7 of Cups that you always seem to be looking at paintings, use that. This way, over time, you'll weave together what you offer the card and what the card offers you until they are indistinguishable. You will be *living the poem*.

Here's space for a few samples:

• Card I Drew: _____

• Spell: _____

_____

_____

• Card I Drew: _____

• Spell: _____

_____

_____

• Card I Drew: _____

• Spell: _____

_____

_____

Assignment 8.2
DIY Adventure Spell

This spell is an incredibly powerful practice, not an everyday practice like Card of the Day. It is a specialized reading for getting you from where you are to where you want to be.

Now that you speak fluent tarot, you're going to deliberately choose a card that eloquently describes your current situation—particularly whatever facet of your situation dissatisfies you. That's Card A. Then you're going to deliberately choose a card that eloquently describes where you would like to be. Once you've decided on these two cards—these agents of your present and future—you're going to shuffle them back into the deck, find them again, and randomly choose from the cards between them to make a bridge from Card A to Card B.

The thing is, you don't know where Card A and Card B are going to end up. They might end up right next to each other; they might end up seventy-six cards apart. That's symbolically meaningful. If they end up really far apart, maybe you've got a bit of a journey ahead of you before you can realize your goal. If they end up shoulder to shoulder, maybe you're nearly there.

Either way, you're going to devise a magical shortcut by choosing just a few cards from the stack between the two points. These will show you the signposts along your journey—changes you must make or things you must accomplish. Think of them as the kind of instructions the hero of a fairy tale gets at the beginning of her adventure: "When you get to the crossroads, you will encounter a magical stag who will ask you for a handful of salt. In return, it will give you one of its antlers. Do not lose the antler!"

The DIY Adventure Spell gives you an awesome power to steer yourself toward whatever it is you desire in this life. *Use it wisely*, all right?

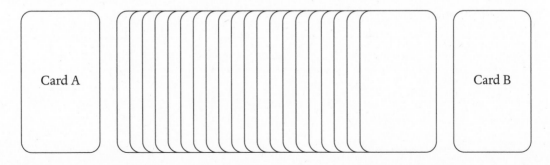

Instructions

Here's the basic procedure:

1 | Choose a card that represents where you are (Card A) and where you want to be (Card B). That's right, choose them *on purpose*.

2 | Then, shuffle those two cards back into the deck. Shuffle really well so that you have no idea whether Card A and Card B are going to end up right next to each other, seventy-six cards apart, or somewhere in between.

3 | Once you've finished shuffling, place the cards faceup, keeping the deck in order, and find the two cards you chose. Pick up all the cards that lie between Card A and Card B and make a neat pile; set it facedown. (You can set the "outside" cards—the ones that don't lie between A and B—aside. You won't be needing those.)

4 | Time to find your steps! Place Card A and B faceup. Between them, place the cards that were between them, facedown in a line. Spread these cards out. You're going to choose a finite, manageable number of steps to get from Card A to Card B. I find three steps usually works pretty well, though you can do more or fewer depending on what you think you can handle. Once you've decided, randomly draw those cards from the line of facedown cards.

5 | Read your adventure! You've just designed a step-by-step program for getting from Card A to Card B. Follow the steps and see what happens!

Just by way of example, here are some hypothetical cards you might use for Cards A and B. But I encourage you to come up with your own!

Current Situation	Card A		Ideal Future Situation	Card B
Stuckness	8 of Swords	→	Freedom	The Sun
Sorrow	3 of Swords	→	Joy	9 of Pentacles
Conflict	5 of Wands	→	Peace	4 of Swords
Addiction	The Devil	→	Release	The Star
Poverty	5 of Pentacles	→	Wealth	10 of Pentacles

Current Situation	Card A		Ideal Future Situation	Card B
		→		

_____

_____

_____

_____

_____

_____

_____

_____

_____

_____

_____

_____

Assignment 8.3
Tree of Life Spell

The Tree of Life is the fundamental conceptual structure of Kabbalah, a form of Jewish mysticism concerned with the creation of the world. This spell uses the Golden Dawn's correspondences for the Tree of Life as a kind of scaffolding.

If you are unfamiliar with Kabbalah, all you need to know for this exercise is that there are ten *sephiroth* (spheres or circles that represent stages in Creation), which correspond to the numbers Ace through 10 in the minor arcana. You can use the Ace through 10 keywords you developed in chapter 3 to get a sense of what each of those stages represents. There are also twenty-two paths between those sephiroth, which correspond to the twenty-two major arcana.

Because the Golden Dawn society was fascinated with the Tree of Life, every card in the deck has a place in this structure—the court cards too—but we are going to concern ourselves only with the numeric minor arcana and the major arcana. You're going to choose two numeric minor arcana cards with different numbers to represent where you are and where you want to be. Then you're going to determine the path/major arcanum that runs between them, and you're going to write a spell based on that.

You may notice some numbers don't connect directly to other numbers. For example, if you want to jump from Ace to 10, you'd have to travel from Ace to 6 (the path of the High Priestess), 6 to 9 (Temperance), and 9 to 10 (World). From 2 to 5, you'd have go from 2 to 3 (Empress), and 3 to 5 (Chariot)—or from 2 to 4 to 5. Just as in life, some places are harder to get to than others from where you are! But that doesn't mean you can't do it.

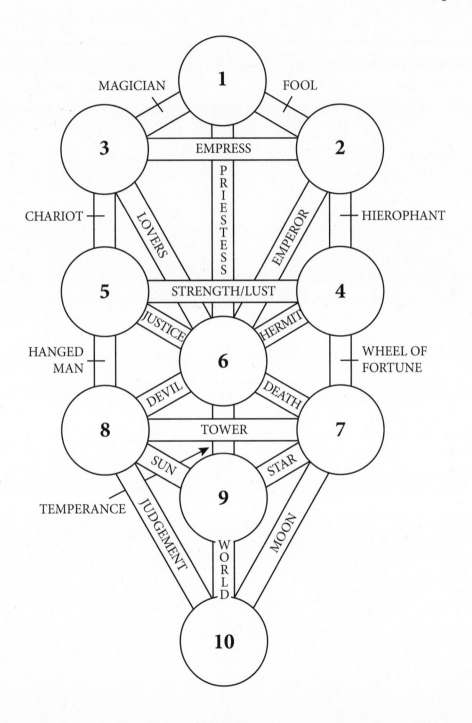

Instructions

1 | Pick two minor arcana cards that together represent a change you'd like to make in yourself. Make sure to choose cards that have different numbers. For example, suppose I want to stop being so distracted all the time and be able to focus better. I might use the 7 of Swords and the 8 of Pentacles to represent "distraction" and "focus."

  • Cards I Chose:

  1. _____

  2. _____

2 | Locate the relevant numbers (in this case, number 7 and number 8) on the diagram. What major lies between them? Pull this major out and set it between the 7 of Swords and 8 of Pentacles. If you've chosen two cards that don't connect by a single path, you may need to use more cards, as if you're changing buses!

  • Additional Card(s): _____

3 | Look at the three (or more) cards and devise a spell that captures the change you want to make, using the major as the key to unlocking that change.
    For example:

Demons of distraction, fall!
The air is cleared. The work is all.

_____

_____

_____

Assignment 8.4

The Unweaving Fate Spell

For this exercise, I'm going to introduce you to the idea of the paralogical metaphor.

Stay with me here!

You already know all about metaphors, right? You use metaphors when you use a word or phrase to refer to something other than its literal meaning. If I say "The grocery store was a zoo today," you know I don't mean that there were actual chimpanzees waltzing down aisle seven. I mean that it was busy, that chaos had the upper hand, and it's possible some people were acting like literal animals.

But what if I say "The grocery store was a coral reef today"? Or "The grocery store was a baritone sax today"? What does that mean? I have no idea! What about "The hammer is the casserole of the toolbox"? Blank stares. These are *paralogical metaphors*, also known as *absolute metaphors* or *anti-metaphors*. They defy sense. They are open-ended and undecodable. They challenge our assumptions; our relationship to sense-making and reality. And that makes them a powerful magical tool.

In the *Book of Taliesin*, which dates from the sixth century BC, there's a famous passage. It goes like this:

> I have been a blue salmon,
> I have been a dog, a stag, a roebuck on the mountain,
> A stock, a spade, an axe in the hand,
> A stallion, a bull, a buck,
> I was reaped and placed in an oven;
> I fell to the ground when I was being roasted
> And a hen swallowed me.
> For nine nights was I in her crop.
> I have been dead, I have been alive.
> I am Taliesin.[19]

It could be a literal account of the magical transformations undergone by the legendary bard Taliesin—the story of a human repeatedly taking on new forms and shapes. Or it could

---

19 | Gwyneth Lewis and Rowan Williams, trans., *The Book of Taliesin: Poems of Warfare and Praise in an Enchanted Britain* (New York: Penguin Classics, 2020).

be a way of saying the bard's nature is protean and infinite. It sounds like a boast, a war-cry, a spell. Whatever it is, it's *powerful*.

And in this exercise, we're going to do what Taliesin did.

Instructions

1 | Shuffle and draw a card randomly. Before turning it over, close your eyes and breathe deeply for a moment. Forget who you are or who you are expected to be.

2 | Turn the card over and declare, "I am [the name of the card]."

3 | Start looking for notable features in the card, then continue: "I am the X." "I am the Y." "I am the Z." Do this at least half a dozen times. You don't have to restrict yourself to just what you see, either. Imagine the card is three-dimensional and in motion, and you've stepped into it. You get to use all your senses.

4 | Conclude by once again declaring, "I am [the name of the card]."

Example:

I am the 5 of Wands.
I am the broad blue sky.
I am the rough terrain.
I am the leaf sprouting from the living wood.
I am the brown shoe that doesn't match.
I am the fist that grasps and strikes.
I am the taste of sweat.
I am the contest and I am the dance.
I am the furious blow of your glance.
I am the 5 of Wands.

You can do this in writing, or just speak it out loud. You can do it many times with the same card, or just once with many cards. You can do it for your Card of the Day. You can do it with a magazine cover, or your favorite painting, or the landscape you walk through on your way to the mailbox.

Unlike every other exercise in this book, this one is not about building meaning, but *unraveling old webs of meaning* so you are free to make new ones. If, at the end of it, you feel no wiser than you began—if, in fact, your head feels strangely, almost refreshingly, empty—then you did it right. Be like Taliesin! Stop making sense!

• • • • • •

Assignment 8.5

Sympathetic and Apotropaic Magic

In your chapter 4 final assignment, "Walk the Walk," you drew a card and you found a way to enact the image. Although we didn't make a big deal out of it at the time, *this was actually magic*. Rather than simply observing what happened with your card over the course of the day, you found a way to express its nature proactively.

We're going to take it a step further in this exercise. When we step beyond just reading tarot, when we start to live and breathe tarot, we are engaging in acts of co-creation. It's a lot like what happens when we're dreaming: we create and destroy a world even as we live within it. Everything we do has meaning; everything we do is a symbol for something else.

Have you ever been going through something huge, something mythic in your life—you fell in love; broke up with someone; threw the winning pass in the big game; your meme went viral!—and somehow everything in your exterior real life seemed to converge? You walked into a store and you heard a song that seemed to be directly about you; you saw an ad on the subway and it used the *very words you just said* at the big moment, etc. My Jungian friends might say that in that moment, you were "constellating an archetype"—connecting with something much larger than yourself and expressing or embodying it. My friends in vodou might say you were being "spirit-ridden."

When we work with tarot, we court these synchronicities. Ever on the lookout for added meaning, we become the heroes of our own lives. And when they don't explicitly happen to us—when Fate seems to have forgotten us, when Providence fails to provide—we *make them happen*. That is the principle behind sympathetic magic.

In this exercise, you are going to engage in a form of sympathetic magic known as *apotropaic magic*. That's "turning away" or "warding off" magic. I suggest you use a card that you feel a bit uneasy about. Some obvious candidates are the 10 of Swords, or the Tower, or the 5 of Pentacles, but there might well be others that set you off. Maybe the Knight of Swords makes you feel nervous, or the 4 of Cups makes you feel queasy and dissatisfied.

Maybe it happens to be your Card of the Day, or maybe you've just decided to work with it deliberately. It doesn't matter. Whichever it is, doing this exercise puts you in the driver's seat. You never have to let a card just happen to you. Because you, my friend, are a co-creator of the Universe! Live the poem!

Instructions

1 | Choose a card that makes you feel uneasy—one that makes you flinch or wince a bit when you get it.

2 | Look at the imagery closely. What symbols do you see? What analogues do they have in ordinary life? Cups are easy, since bowls and mugs and glasses are everywhere. Wands could be anything sticklike or wooden, from tree branches to drumsticks to chopsticks to rolling pins. Swords could be anything sharp. Pentacles could be anything round. Pay particular attention to number, since tarot likes to count.

3 | Design an action around the imagery. Be creative! Have fun! Some apotropaic actions I've undertaken:

- Buying ten needles, or observing the Japanese custom of Hari-Kuyō (burying used needles) for the 10 of Swords
- Cracking an egg for omelets for the Tower
- Fixing a lock on the front door for the 5 of Pentacles

4 | Perform the action. Declare, "The requirements have been fulfilled!"

5 | Write up your results in a paragraph or two.

6 | Have a good laugh, take a deep breath, and go about your day, knowing that card has done what it needed to do.

_____

_____

_____

_____

_____

_____

_____

Chapter 8 Final Assignment
Make a Tarot Talisman

Over the last several years, I've been really interested in what the Western occult tradition calls "image magic." Usually, that means medieval and Renaissance astrological image magic, of the kind propounded by Heinrich Cornelius Agrippa von Nettesheim and Marsilio Ficino. But you can find image magic in lots of other texts beloved of magicians: for example, the *Picatrix* (eleventh century), or the *Greek Magical Papyri* (first century). You could argue that the Lascaux cave paintings are image magic, or that the giant heads on Rapa Nui (Easter Island) are image magic.

Personally, I believe that any time you work with images with magical intent, you are engaging in a form of image magic. And what is tarot, if not a set of images invested with magical intent? These are images that can receive, project, focus, and transmute the will of the person using them. You may not have the resources or experience to make a full-blown Renaissance-style astrological talisman, created when the moon is rising in the first decan of Cancer, made out of mother-of-pearl, and quenched in frog juice.

However, you can certainly put something together that has layers of meaningful symbolism, is created in a meaningful way at a meaningful time, and is charged with personally meaningful intent. It may be hard to accept, in a modern materialist context, that such a thing could actually work. But maybe—if you accept the theory behind creating a talisman in the first place—a better question is: *why shouldn't it?*

As documented in my book *36 Secrets: A Decanic Journey through the Minor Arcana of the Tarot*, I created my first crude tarot talisman in 2019, when my daughter and I were headed halfway around the world to visit relatives in Singapore and I was struck with the notion to make 8 of Wands luggage tags. If the 8 of Wands could be counted on to deliver messages and packages, I reasoned, might it not also successfully deliver suitcases? During a Mercury hour a few days before the flight, I took some printouts of the card, stuck them on cardboard with packing tape, wrote our return address on the back, and affixed them to our bags with zip ties.

Well, I have to say, I have never gotten my bags through an airport so fast. Both coming and going (and in between, when we had to manually transfer them through the international gates), they were among the first to make it onto the belt. The customs guys barely looked at them. It was as if they had an invisible guardian shepherding them along with maximum speed and minimum fuss.

Later, I embellished the talisman with seals of Mercury and had them properly printed on indestructible plastic. I also had 8 of Wands key fobs made, and you can get all of that at my Etsy store. But—and this is my point—*nothing's stopping you from making your own!*

So in this exercise, you're going to create your own tarot talisman. You're going to build it in a meaningful way, and then you're going to consecrate it in a ritual of your own devising.

"But I'm not an artist!" I hear you objecting. That's okay—neither am I. You can use tracing paper. You can use Photoshop. You can use scissors and glue and make a collage. You can use found objects.

Of course, if you *are* an artist, you can go to town on this assignment and work with whatever media and techniques you like. Just make sure you start with actual tarot imagery, and keep that source material in mind as you work.

Instructions

The way I see it, four elements go into the making of a talisman: intent, including Logos (the discriminating, conscious, rational intellect) and Eros (the connecting, unconscious, desire nature in the psyche); symbolic imagery; materia; and timing. All are necessary to "enliven" your talisman, which you might think of more as a living being than an inert object.

1 | **Articulate Your Intent.** What are you trying to accomplish? Whatever it is, it probably has a certain feeling about it, and it likely can also be expressed (or approximated) in words. The words are your Logos: your statement of intent; your words or argument. So, write down what you want. Clarity and concision are good, but it's also good to try and make it beautiful. Make it something you can memorize easily—and when you're done, that's your spell. Logos could also include any words you use to call upon a corresponding power, if you're doing that (whether it's Hermes, or the Fates, or your great-grandmother who was a *strega*).

There's another aspect to intention, and that is *eros*. Eros is the accompanying feeling of excitement and victory you get when something you want is about to come to pass. Not to be confused with the nervousness of *Am I doing this right?* or the fear of not getting what you want. You could be feeling pride, if what you're aiming for is fame and success. It could be the feeling of being in love, if you're looking for a romantic partner. (It could even be righteous anger, I suppose, if you're trying to bring down someone who's wronged you.) Whatever it is, allow yourself to experience the feeling as you work to create your talisman. Breathe deep and relax into it. You can even put on music that gets you in the right mood.

2 | **Choose Symbolic Imagery.** For imagery, the obvious place to start is with the tarot card itself. You can scan it or trace it, snap a picture and print it out, or work on the actual card itself if you don't mind breaking up your deck. You can use any part of the card, or you might use the whole thing. I find the black-and-white line images of the Rider-Waite-Smith really helpful for this. Then, add layers to it using any of the following:

- **Symbols:** You can use shapes that have symbolic meaning, like hearts or dollar signs. You can use images that are based on correspondences (like the hoopoe bird associated with the Capricorn I decan), or tradition (like wedding rings, a wrapped present, a paycheck, or an MVP trophy).

- **Color:** You can use colors based on correspondences (Jupiter = blue, for example) or tradition (US currency is green!).

- **Custom Sigils:** You can make up your own sigil based on your statement of intent. There are lots of ways to transform a written statement into a sigil.[20] Most involve taking out redundant letters and/or vowels and mashing the remaining letter forms into a mysterious-looking graphic.

- **Traditional Sigils, Seals, and Signs:** Borrow freely from magical traditions: runes, words written in languages not your own, planetary seals from grimoires. I suggest you don't worry too much about appropriation here. Magic has always been inherently syncretic, a chaotic blend of every tradition there is or ever was. And this is private magic, not something you're going to post about on social media and then have to deal with offended followers. Do your research, and if the meaningfulness of the symbol holds up under scrutiny, use it. The foreignness of the image—its lack of familiarity to you, the practitioner—can actually be part of the magic.

- **Personal Symbols:** Have a thing for crows? Really love ferns? Obsessed with mica? Is there a funny way you used to write your initials as a kid? Consider adding that in too, as a kind of personal signature. For that matter, your signature might belong in there too.

20 | I recommend Gordon White's chaos magic–based posts to start (https://runesoup.com/2012/03/ultimate-sigil-magic-guide/), or you can use one of the innumerable sigil generators now available online.

3 | **Select the Materia.** Materia is just the physical stuff your talisman is made of. Paper is completely fine for this exercise, but if you are crafty and you want to take your talisman to the next level, you could add in other meaningful substances. You could use fancy colored paper, parchment, or papyrus. You could work in leather, cloth, or wood. If you're a jeweler, you could inscribe metal or add beads.

Besides whatever substrate the image goes on, you can bring in other materia for your ritual. You can anoint your image with oil or perfume. You can bring in natural objects, like leaves or flowers or stones. You can offer wine or incense. You may want to incorporate what rootworkers call "personal concerns" (hair, blood, or other intimate substances), but that's up to you.

4 | **Choose the Timing.** Choose an appropriate time to finish and "charge" your talisman. Traditional talismans pay attention to what's going on in the sky. This could be astrological: when the moon is in Taurus in the third mansion, for example. It could be solar or lunar: sunrise, at the full moon, or as the moon wanes for things you're trying to get rid of, or solar observances like the spring equinox or winter solstice. Or it could be calendrical: Thursday is the day of Jupiter, for example, and you could use the planetary hour of Jupiter (sunrise, or the eighth planetary hour of the day).

I'd also argue that you could choose non-esoteric, personally meaningful times, like your birthday. Or Christmas. Or the New Year. Or your anniversary. Or Monday morning when the stock market opens.

5 | **Do the Ritual.** At the meaningful time of your choosing, go to a meaningful place (an altar, or wherever it is that you want the desired outcome to take place). You can use your quarter-calling or banishing ritual from chapter 7, if you like. Take out the talisman and any corresponding materia; light your candle or incense or anything else you may have. Call down and praise any powers you want to preside over the talisman. Talk to the talisman about what you want. Say your spell, multiple times if you like. You can sing or chant if that feels good. Finally, say thanks and dismiss whatever spirits you've called on. Or you can simply thank the talisman itself and give it a kiss!

6 | **Follow Through Afterward.** Commit your spell to memory and, while holding the talisman, recite it each morning for at least a week. (You can absolutely recite it more than once a day, and you can absolutely do this for more than a week, if you like.) Carry the talisman in your pocket or your wallet or your phone case—i.e., as close to you as you can manage. After a week, write up your results.

_____

_____

_____

_____

_____

_____

_____

_____

Some Sources for Symbols and Correspondences

Three Books of Occult Philosophy by Heinrich Cornelius Agrippa von Nettesheim

The Rulership Book: A Directory of Astrological Correspondences by Rex E. Bills

Tarot Correspondences: Ancient Secrets for Everyday Readers by T. Susan Chang

Cunningham's Encyclopedia of Magical Herbs by Scott Cunningham

Picatrix: The Classic Medieval Handbook of Astrological Magic by John Michael Greer and Christopher Warnock

777 and Other Qabalistic Writings of Aleister Crowley by Aleister Crowley

The Western Mysteries: An Encyclopedic Guide to the Sacred Languages & Magickal Systems of the World by David Allen Hulse

Tarot and Magic by Donald Michael Kraig

The Magical and Ritual Use of Perfumes by Richard Alan Miller and Iona Miller

The Complete Magician's Tables by Stephen Skinner

Secrets of Planetary Magic by Christopher Warnock

The Magician's Companion: A Practical & Encyclopedic Guide to Magical & Religious Symbolism by Bill Whitcomb

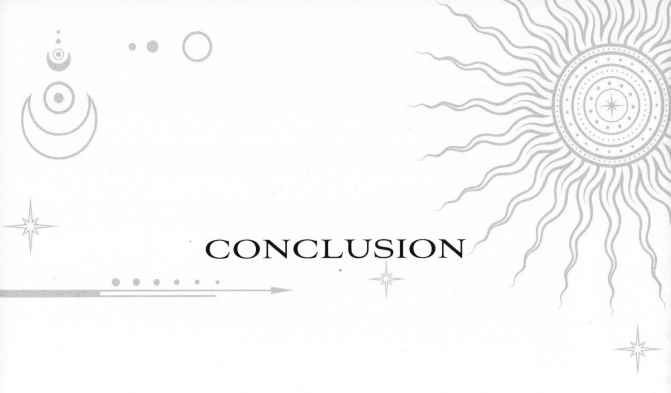

CONCLUSION

What a long way you've come from the first day you took a chance on this book! By now, I hope, the cards—those seventy-eight beloved children of Fortuna—have become cherished companions, and a part of your daily life.

Because you live tarot, that glass of cool water on a hot day is your Ace of Cups.

Because you live tarot, the 6 of Pentacles goes with you when you walk into the job interview, reminding you that opportunities are everywhere you look.

Because you live tarot, when you draw the Tower on a stormy evening and hear a crack of thunder and a flash of lightning illuminates your dining room, you rejoice. "The requirements have been fulfilled!" you exclaim.

Tarot is more than a hobby and more than a game. It's more than a spooky interface with a spirit world. Tarot is a way of life! What's on the surface of those colorful images is only the beginning. Just beneath their printed surface, the cards contain the whole world.

Every card is a storehouse, a repository for your lived experience. The World holds the day you stood by your best friend's side, squeezing her hand as she gave birth to her daughter. The 3 of Wands holds the day you went on that hike up the mountain and decided to quit smoking for good this time. And the Queen of Swords holds the memory of your sharp-tongued Aunt Trish (may she rest in peace) and all her terrible, hilarious tales.

Every card is a doorway, alive with potential. Maybe you haven't yet gone on that cross-country road trip you always wanted to, but the Chariot tells you you *could*. Maybe you've not yet learned to draw, or scry in a crystal ball, or record your dreams, but the 7 of Cups says that's still a part of you.

And on those days when you are feeling small and unimportant, tarot gives you a way to renegotiate your limits. It gives you a way to extend your boundaries and a way to reignite hope. Because the cards are a metaphor for the whole world as well as a metaphor for you. When you hunt inside tarot, reaching with all your senses for what something might signify, you aren't just discovering meaning. You are *making it*. Tarot is infinite, and so are you.

You are the flaming arrow that sets the woods alight.

You are a creature of swirling depths and hidden treasures.

You are the voice of the restless wind.

You are the lockbox and you are the key.

You are the cards and the cards are you.

Live the poem!

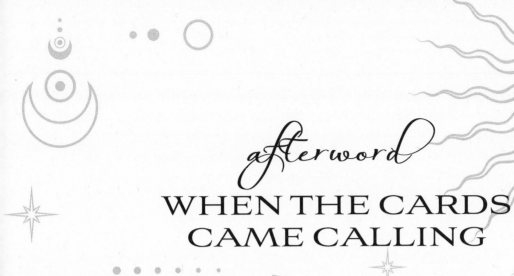

afterword

WHEN THE CARDS
CAME CALLING

This book is about you, not about me. It's about how the tarot comes to life for you, in the way you pour your coffee in the morning, or the way you go about your first day on the job, or the way your cat snuggles up to you when you're reading in bed. It's about the living, breathing web of metaphor all around you, and the way you catch glimpses of it in the cards. It's about your heroic adventure and your mythic self. It's about how tarot came into your life and changed it forever.

That said, before we part ways, perhaps you would like to hear how tarot came into mine.

Divination in a Dorm Room

The first time I saw a tarot deck up close was in the fall of 1987, when I arrived at college. I shared a suite with three other first years, but Mel H. lived next door to us in her own single room. Mel seemed to know who she was; voluble, performative, sociable, with a boyfriend she totally eclipsed. She had a steady blue-gray gaze, a ready laugh, and she was constantly rolling up her sleeves. She liked to describe herself as "Rubenesque," and she was the kind of person you could go to for a condom on the night you lost your virginity. She also taught me to use my first computer mouse, back then when such things were new.

Mel had a tarot deck, and she knew how to read it. Needless to say, this made her single room a mecca within the dorm. During my three years at Harvard (I started out as a sophomore),

I never met anyone else who read cards. It's not that it would've been frowned upon; Harvard turned out to be a place where quirkiness was an asset, since it was a given that everyone was brilliant. But it also seemed that everyone else had a sense where they were headed in life. What would they need tarot for?

Mel and I were friends, but like everyone else, I was constantly angling for a reading. The subject was *always* men; or, more accurately, boys. To this day, I don't remember a single detail of those readings. I do remember walking through the snow up to the vintage store in North Cambridge, where they had a Dalí Tarot. Several of us had put together funds, and we bought it for Mel. Honestly, it was the least we could do.

It never occurred to me, in those days, that I might read tarot myself. Mel's deck was a Marseille tarot, with unadorned suit emblems on the minor arcana. Learning and memorizing seventy-eight meanings seemed like a mathematical tour de force. And how did it work, anyway? The whole idea was inscrutable metaphysically, and probably too much work intellectually. I got back to the proper business of college—studying, being broke, and worrying about boys—and did not bother my head about tarot again for nearly a decade.

First Deck

By 1997 I was well immersed in the proper business of young adulthood—working, being broke, and worrying about boys—and uncertainty was creeping up on me. From the outside, I seemed to have it together as a thoughtful young book editor at an academic press. But inside, I was bored, lonely, and chafing at the bit. The cure for this restlessness varied from year to year: sometimes I cooked elaborate, wine-soaked meals for one. For a while I went ballroom dancing almost every night, and at another point I started learning the saxophone. There were times I did all of the above; and of course there was the endless parade of boys, who were starting to look deceptively like men.

But one Saturday, when I was sitting alone (again) at dinner, pondering one more impenetrable dissertation and brooding over Johnny the tango dancer, I finally realized I'd just had it. Had it with what? I couldn't have told you, but in retrospect, I think I would say it was the apparent meaninglessness of it all. Every move I had made up to this point had made sense in some way, and yet life still seemed sterile. How could I find work I truly enjoyed? What exactly was success, anyway? Where would I find love?

Now tarot, unlike my life choices to date, made no sense at all. How could meaning arise from the pure chaos of seventy-eight randomly shuffled cards? With a blithe disregard for the laws of causality, tarot seemed to wholeheartedly embrace the very uncertainty I so feared. Tarot could pull meaning literally out of thin air. Maybe I could too.

I've kept a diary every day since I was twelve. That very Saturday night I finished off the page in a state of maudlin, self-serious exhaustion:

> May 2, 1997
> "I plan tomorrow to learn to read tarot and buy my first cards. Because there is only so much uncertainty I can live with, and I must keep silent on my dreams."

Ouch. It makes me cringe a little, now. But I followed through, and it changed my life.

> May 3, 1997
> "A good day. I did indeed buy my first tarot deck—Rider-Waite—and sat in the restaurant Pisces learning how to use them…"

(My ascendant's in Pisces, though that was the last thing on my mind when I walked into that now-defunct restaurant.)

Several boring thoughts about boys followed. But what I most remember from that day, when I started my tarot journey in earnest, was that the first card of my own I ever laid eyes on was the Queen of Swords. I saw her determined profile, her raised arm, her butterfly crown, her sharp sword, and a light shudder passed down my spine.

I didn't know much about tarot, but I'd read enough to know that of the four Queens, it was this one—the sharp-edged, single, up-in-her-head woman who loved to dance—that I most recognized. Not the frank and friendly Queen of Wands; not the blonde and empathic Queen of Cups; not the capable, house-proud Queen of Pentacles. No, for me it was the Queen of Swords (aka the Queen of Spades, or *Pique Dame*, or Black Maria), and the more I learned of her forbidding past, the better I liked her.

On the third day, I drew a Card of the Day for the first time. It was, needless to say, the Queen of Swords.

Infinity on a Train

Spine-tingling synchronicities are normal for tarot, I would soon learn. But what is synchronicity, really? Jung defined synchronicity as *meaningful coincidence*. Coincidences happen all the time. What makes them meaningful is the fact that we *notice*. This noticing—this active participation on the part of the subjective Self—lies at the heart of divination.

In that first flush of awe and fascination in 1997, I wondered what everyone wonders: *Who is behind this?!* Surely something external—God, the Universe, Fate, the Devil—had to be causing the cards to fall in such an uncanny way, because I wasn't making it up.

Twenty-five years later, I think I have an answer: it's what Jung would have called the Self. But I remain awed and fascinated because the Self is so much larger than I guessed at the time; so unconstrained by the perceived, three-dimensional world of T. Susan Chang. As it turns out, this Self *was* making it up all along. But—in the immortal words of Dumbledore: "Why on earth should that mean that it is not real?"[21]

Back then, though, my understanding of the cards was skeletal. And like every new tarot reader, I banged my head against the wall trying to come up with meanings. I could physically *feel* the meaning present in the cards, like a buzz going through my hands as I held the deck, but I couldn't put it into words. If the Ace of Swords came up again and again and again, it was plain to see that something big was going on, but *what could it mean?* Like a rookie astrologer seeing an eclipse forming a partile conjunction to someone's ascendant, all I could do was point excitedly at the cards as a little speech bubble filled with exclamation points appeared over my head.

It was frustrating, and when the cards were less dramatic—say, 4 of Cups and 7 of Pentacles and Page of Swords—you couldn't even do the pointing part.

One afternoon a few months in, I was on a train on my way to Cape Cod, diligently staring at the cards laid out on my tray table and coming up completely dry. *This is ridiculous*, I said to myself. *Why am I even wasting my time? Why don't I go home and apply to graduate school or something worthwhile?*

The sun beat down on my left ear, and the tracks were loud beneath the wheels. I shuffled the cards back together. *Give me one reason why I shouldn't give up right now*, I thought. I drew one card facedown. And then, just in case, I drew one more. I closed my eyes, laid my hands on the hot tray table, and slowly turned the cards over.

It was the Magician and Strength, looking up at me from their twin yellow rooms, each bedecked with roses, each with an infinity sign over their head; each an image of power and possibility. I didn't know about the Magician's connection to Mercury, or the 8 of Pentacles, or the Emerald Tablet of Hermes Trismegistus, all of which would later become important to

---

21 | J. K. Rowling, *Harry Potter and the Deathly Hallows* (New York: Scholastic, 2007).

me. I didn't know that I would come to associate Strength with (among other things) public achievement and being in the spotlight.

But as I looked at those cards, the speech bubble above my head began to fill up with exclamation points again. For the moment, that was enough.

Life of the Party

Just about every tarot reader goes through a "friends and family" phase, whether or not they eventually turn pro. Mine lasted eighteen years, though yours doesn't have to.

For a little while, I read tarot for tips once a week in a café in Hell's Kitchen, which was a marvelous experience.[22] Such drama! I fulfilled the American Tarot Association's requirements and received a "Certified Professional Tarot Reader" certificate, which attested to the good intentions of all concerned, though not much else. Despite the title, I was still working my day job, and then I was moving to New England, and then I was raising a family and freelancing as a writer. Tarot formed a distant second to all these obligations.

The cards were always with me, though. I continued to draw a daily card, and I continued to think and dream about tarot. The cards were there the day I posted the personal ad that led me to my husband (Queen of Swords) and the day we got engaged (Queen of Wands); they were on the cover of our wedding program (2 of Cups). On the morning I discovered I was pregnant with our son, I groggily reached my hand out of bed and pulled out the Empress. Each time we went to a dinner or a party, I had a deck in my bag. I didn't mind reading for hours, or the weird sense of floating in outer space afterward. (Which is a thing—exactly why you needed to do the final assignment in chapter 7.)

By now I knew tarot was "real." It was funny, it was helpful, it was weird, and it was wonderful. It helped me understand my first kid, and my second. It got me through the two decades my dad had Alzheimer's and the decade years he lived with us. It advised me through cooking school, and through my career as a food writer, and as a writing instructor, and then as an author. Even during the nine exhausting years when I stopped drawing the daily card, it never failed me if I asked for help. Bit by bit, tarot became a way of life for me. But it surely couldn't be a way of making a living! I mean, who does that?

---

22 | Fully chronicled in "The Fortune Teller's Teacup" in my first book, *A Spoonful of Promises*.

What Was in the Cards

I found out just who did that in the last days of 2014. It was an exceptionally difficult time, when my sister and I were scrambling to find a place for our dad, whose assisted living facility had informed us he needed a "higher level of care." The days were a blur of financial, legal, professional, parental, filial, and educational obligations, and as the New Year approached I found myself in dire need of escape.

On Facebook, I found the group that called itself "Tarot Professionals." *Am I a tarot professional?* I asked myself. The answer was no, but I joined anyway, and it turned out that amongst the professionals there were also tons of curious, interested enthusiasts just like me. Occasionally there was some pedantry or squabbling, but mostly I was glad for the conversation and community.

I started drawing a daily card again that winter, and I was surprised at how much relief it gave me amid the uncertainties. I met people who regularly read for others, people who wrote books about tarot, people who collected decks, and people like me who loved symbolic systems.

I began to invest first energy, then time, then money in tarot. In 2015 I started sewing and selling tarot cases, just for fun. In 2016 I started reading at a local shop, and another Mel came into my life—Mel Meleen, the creator of the Tabula Mundi and Rosetta Tarots. In 2017 we launched the *Fortune's Wheelhouse* esoteric tarot podcast, at which point I also started making and selling perfumes based on the astrological correspondences I'd just learned for the podcast. By this point it was clear that whether or not I thought it was possible to make a living from tarot, that was what was happening. *If I am going to do this insane thing*, I thought to myself, *I am going to do the sh*t out of it.*

In 2018, I released *Tarot Correspondences*, a reference guide for all the esoteric systems embedded in Golden Dawn–based tarot, because I couldn't find one and I needed it. I also launched the Living Tarot online tarot course. In 2020, as Covid closed in around everyone, I hunkered down and wrote *36 Secrets* (my book on the minor arcana) and then *Tarot Deciphered*, co-written with Mel.

Today, tarot is woven into the fabric of my life. My day begins with the daily draw, a half-hour ritual that includes planetary devotions, ancestor reverence, and a spell I write based on whatever cards I get. During the day, there are books to write, clients to read for, students to teach, tarot cases to sew.

It's tarot I turn to when I am upset or confused. It's tarot on my screensaver, tarot on the walls of my office (ten Wheels of Fortune!), tarot in my dreams. It's tarot that claims the last waking moment of my day, when I sit with the diary I've written for forty years and decode whatever it was the cards were trying to tell me that morning. Every day that I get to shuffle a deck and see what the cards have to say, I think I am the luckiest person in the whole world.

And now that the cards have come calling for you, I hope that you feel just the same.

TSC

Midsummer, 2022
Leverett, Massachusetts

RECOMMENDED
RESOURCES

I love books, and I know you do too. Why, you're holding one right now! But I have mixed feelings about using books when you're just starting out as a card reader.

We've all had the experience of opening up a deck, extracting the Little White Book, and poring over it as if it contained the secrets of the Universe. Or maybe you found a proper-sized book of tarot meanings that you liked. There are lots of really good ones out there—maybe you even have one of mine! But when you sit down to do a reading, you find yourself turning to the book to look up a card. And then another. And another. Before you know it, what you're doing looks a lot like reading a book, and not so much like reading cards. Oh no!

I can't tell you how many times I ask someone if they read tarot, and they say, "I've had a deck for a couple of years, but I'm still a beginner. I still have to look up the meanings in the book." Why do so many of us get stalled at this stage? Why do we feel we have to turn to a book for the "right" meaning?

I think it's because we think we ought to memorize the cards, as if they were vocabulary in a foreign language, or maybe the periodic table. But tarot is *infinite* in scope! It's everything you know *plus* everything you can imagine and everything you can't! How can any book define that for you? Even the best book of meanings can't tell you every mystery the 5 of Swords has to offer.

So, as you've seen in this book, my strategy has been to start with what you know. Hopefully, if you've made it even as far as chapter 4, you've got a seed of meaning for every one of

239

those seventy-eight cards. You have a rough idea of what each card looks like in ordinary life, and more importantly, what each card *feels* like.

That initial meaning is like a seed crystal, or the grit in an oyster. Around that tiny grain, layer after layer of meaning will grow until you carry the tarot upon your person like a string of cosmic pearls! Sometimes meaning will announce itself like the blaring trumpet on Judgement Day. Sometimes meaning will creep in on little cat feet, like the fog, as Carl Sandburg puts it.[23] Meaning will arrive in dreams and when you're reading for strangers and friends. And above all, meaning will arrive every day, in large and small ways, after you've drawn your daily card.

No book—not the Little White Book, not the Bible, not this book—contains the secrets of the Universe. But you know who does? You.

Having said that, let's talk about what books can do for you.

When to Read Books When You're Reading Cards

Here's my opinion: the worst possible time to grab a book is when you're in the middle of a reading. You have an important question, you maybe have someone sitting right in front of you, you have images and context. You have empathy, speech, and a highly functional right brain. That's all you need for a reading! Reaching for a book will only deactivate the wise, intuitive pattern detector that lives inside you. It would be like trying to describe a sky full of stars by calculating the percentage of helium and hydrogen in each one. Accurate? Maybe, but not the point.

That said, I think there are two great times to use a book, or even *lots* of books, when you're learning tarot:

1 | **To supplement your Card of the Day.** When you draw your Card of the Day, at some level you'll be looking for connections to it all day long, even if your awareness of the card is just a distant subroutine somewhere in the back of your brain. If you have time after you draw, read up on meanings for that card, or listen to a card-by-card podcast like *Fortune's Wheelhouse* while you're driving or doing chores. That will help you keep your eye out for synchronicities. As you notice them, your mind will be effortlessly banking that information for future use.

23 | Carl Sandburg, "Fog," Poetry Foundation, accessed January 6, 2023, https://www.poetryfoundation.org /poems/45032/fog-56d2245d7b36c.

2 | **After a reading, in the "post-game."** There's no substitute for that first, context-rich impression when you see two or more cards together. But *after* that, there's no harm in revisiting the reading and using whatever reference materials you have to add extra layers and depth to what you learned. It could be just a few minutes after, or it could be the next day when you're looking at the picture or notes you took of the reading. (I hope you took a picture! I hope you took notes!)

If you've been studying esoteric systems, some of what you've learned is bound to inform what you said in the reading. Afterward is also a good time to spell out and excavate any esoteric information. It's when you can do your Kabbalah calculus ("Look! you got the Death card and the Moon, and they're both connected to Netzach!") or your astrology deep dive ("You have a stellium at 27 degrees Gemini? That just *happens* to be in the shadow decan of the Queen of Cups, which you got over *here*, and here's why that might be important.") If your friend or client doesn't speak those languages, don't make them (or yourself) crazy trying to explain. Just go ahead and translate. ("Death and the Moon? They both have to do with how we feel about the things we seek in this life." Or, "The Queen of Cups knows a lot about self-sacrifice, and I bet you do too.")

I think that correspondences are like scales for a musician. You practice them every day, you lie in bed making sense of the cycle of fifths in your head, you internalize the fingering. But then, when it comes to concert time, you forget all of that and just play. The scales are still there, but they form an infrastructure that supports your performance. Correspondences (and reference reading generally) are an infrastructure that lets you fly in a reading.

Books on Tarot Generally

If you're just getting started on your tarot journey with a Rider-Waite-Smith deck and you want to supplement what you're doing with your daily draw and the work you're doing with *The Living Tarot*, you can find some excellent seed crystals for meaning in Rachel Pollack's *Seventy-Eight Degrees of Wisdom* and Mary Greer's *Tarot for Yourself*. If you're a traditionalist, you may want Arthur Edward Waite's *Pictorial Key to the Tarot*, which offers brief sketches of what Waite was getting at when he collaborated with Pamela Colman Smith on the deck.

If you're attracted to esoteric systems, you'll likely enjoy the myriad tables and charts in my first book, *Tarot Correspondences*. You may also wish to follow along with the *Fortune's Wheelhouse* podcast, which is free to all and describes the esoteric symbolism of each card in detail, one card per episode. If you prefer your esoteric symbols decoded in print, you'll want *Tarot Deciphered*, by myself and *Fortune's Wheelhouse* co-host Mel Meleen. If you're into historical esotericism, you may wish to explore the roots of Golden Dawn tarot: McGregor Mathers' Book T (found as part of Israel Regardie's "big black book," *The Golden Dawn*, and widely available as a public-domain PDF). Finally, if you're a tarot history buff, there's a terrific recent compendium of nineteenth- and twentieth-century source texts that capture the way English-speaking occultists thought about the cards at the dawn of modern tarot: *The Tarot: A Collection of Secret Wisdom from Tarot's Mystical Origins*.

In the following list, I'm also including some reference works for the Thoth deck (first created in 1944) and the Tarot de Marseille (a tradition of European woodcut decks extending from the seventeenth century to today). Even if you stick with Rider-Waite-Smith-based decks for the entirety of your tarot career, it's worth knowing a little bit about these other decks. They've had a profound influence on the way people read and interpret tarot today, and they will help you extend your understanding of the cards beyond what's on the surface.

Amberstone, Wald, and Ruth Ann Amberstone. *The Secret Language of Tarot*. San Francisco: Weiser Books, 2008.

Chang, T. Susan. *36 Secrets: A Decanic Journey through the Minor Arcana of the Tarot*. N.p.: Anima Mundi Press, 2020.

———. *Tarot Correspondences: Ancient Secrets for Everyday Readers*. Woodbury, MN: Llewellyn Publications, 2018.

Chang, T. Susan, and M. M. Meleen. *Tarot Deciphered: Decoding Esoteric Symbolism in Modern Tarot*. Woodbury, MN: Llewellyn Publications, 2021.

Crowley, Aleister. *The Book of Thoth: A Short Essay on the Tarot of the Egyptians*. York Beach, ME: Weiser Books, 2017.

David, Jean-Michael. *Reading the Marseille Tarot*. Victoria, ASTL: Association for Tarot Studies, 2011.

Decker, Ronald. *The Esoteric Tarot: Ancient Sources Rediscovered in Hermeticism and Cabala*. Wheaton, IL: Quest Books, 2013.

DuQuette, Lon Milo. *Understanding Aleister Crowley's Thoth Tarot*. New ed. Newburyport, MA: Weiser Books, 2017.

Greer, Mary K. *Tarot for Your Self: A Workbook for Personal Transformation*. 2nd ed. Franklin Lakes, NJ: New Page Books, 2002.

Huson, Paul. *Mystical Origins of the Tarot: from Ancient Roots to Modern Usage.* Rochester, VT: Destiny Books, 2004.

Katz, Marcus, and Tali Goodwin. *Secrets of the Waite-Smith Tarot: The True Story of the World's Most Popular Tarot.* Woodbury, MN: Llewellyn Publications, 2015.

Kenner, Corrine. *Tarot and Astrology: Enhance Your Readings with the Wisdom of the Zodiac.* Woodbury, MN: Llewellyn Publications, 2011.

Liber Theta: Tarot Symbolism and Divination. Los Angeles: College of Thelema, 2012. https://www.thelema.org/publications/books/LiberT.pdf.

Louis, Anthony. *Tarot Beyond the Basics: Gain a Deeper Understanding of the Meanings Behind the Cards.* Woodbury, MN: Llewellyn Publications, 2014.

Mathers, MacGregor, and Harriet Felkin. *Book T - The Tarot: Comprising Manuscripts N, O, P, Q, R, and an Unlettered Theoricus Adeptus Minor Instruction.* Hermetic Order of the Golden Dawn, 1888. https://benebellwen.files.wordpress.com/2013/02/mathers-and-felkin-golden-dawn-book-t-the-tarot-1888.pdf.

Place, Robert M. *The Tarot, Magic, Alchemy, Hermeticism, and Neoplatonism.* 3rd ed. Saugerties, NY: Hermes Publications, 2017.

Pollack, Rachel. *Seventy-Eight Degrees of Wisdom.* New York: HarperCollins Publishers, 1997.

Porterfield, Charles. *A Deck of Spells: Hoodoo Playing Card Magic in Rootwork and Conjure.* Forestville, CA: Lucky Mojo Curio Company, 2015.

Powell, Robert, trans. *Meditations on the Tarot: A Journey into Christian Hermeticism.* New York: Jeremy P. Tarcher/Putnam, 2002.

Renée, Janina. *Tarot Spells.* St. Paul, MN: Llewellyn Publications, 2000.

The Tarot: A Collection of Secret Wisdom from Tarot's Mystical Origins. New York: St. Martin's Essentials, 2021.

Waite, Arthur Edward, and Pamela Colman Smith. *The Pictorial Key to the Tarot: Being Fragments of a Secret Tradition Under the Veil of Divination.* Stamford, CT: US Games Systems, 2001.

Basic Astrology

This is an admittedly idiosyncratic list. Chances are you know a bit of astrology already, or maybe a lot. You may be really into secondary progressions, or Time Lord techniques, or maybe you just read your daily horoscope. The titles below are overviews I've found helpful;

taken together, they are more than sufficient to illuminate the astrology encoded in the Rider-Waite-Smith deck.

Brady, Bernadette. *Predictive Astrology: The Eagle and the Lark*. York Beach, ME: Samuel Weiser, 1999.

Brennan, Chris. *Hellenistic Astrology: The Study of Fate and Fortune*. Denver, CO: Amor Fati Publications, 2017.

Coppock, Austin. *36 Faces: The History, Astrology, and Magic of the Decans*. Hercules, CA: Three Hands Press, 2014.

Nicholas, Chani. *You Were Born for This: Astrology for Radical Self-Acceptance*. New York: Harper One, 2020.

Oken, Alan. *Alan Oken's Complete Astrology: The Classic Guide to Modern Astrology*. Lake Worth, FL: Ibis Press, 2006.

Taylor, Carole. *Astrology: Using the Wisdom of the Stars in Your Everyday Life*. New York: DK Publishing, 2018.

Basic Hermetic Qabalah/Kabbalah and the Tree of Life

If you decide to learn more about the Tree of Life, be aware that there is (1) traditional Kabbalah, directly inherited from Jewish mysticism, and (2) its distant descendant, Hermetic Qabala, constructed by non-Jewish occultists (including the Golden Dawn) and more closely tied to the tarot tradition. If it's spelled with a "Q," that's generally an indication you're talking about the Hermetic tradition.

If you want to get started quickly mapping tarot to the Tree of Life, Rachel Pollack's *The Kabbalah Tree* is a great introduction. If you want to dive deep into the historical origins of traditional Kabbalah, the source texts are the *Sefer Yetzirah* and the *Zohar*; and you will probably want some help from a rabbinical scholar or an academic specialist in Jewish studies to go there.

DuQuette, Lon Milo. *The Chicken Qabalah of Rabbi Lamed Ben Clifford: Dilettante's Guide to What You Do and Do Not Need to Know to Become a Qabalist*. York Beach, ME: Weiser Books, 2010.

Fortune, Dion. *The Mystical Qabalah*. London: Aziloth Books, 2011.

Kaplan, Aryeh. *Sefer Yetzirah: The Book of Creation*. San Francisco: Weiser Books, 1990.

Kliegman, Isabel Radow. *Tarot and the Tree of Life: Finding Everyday Wisdom in the Minor Arcana*. Wheaton, IL: Quest Books, 2013.

Matt, Daniel Chanan, trans. *Zohar: The Book of Enlightenment*. Mahwah, NJ: Paulist Press, 1983.

Pollack, Rachel. *The Kabbalah Tree: A Journey of Balance & Growth*. St. Paul, MN: Llewellyn Publications, 2004.

Regardie, Israel. *A Garden of Pomegranates: Skrying on the Tree of Life*. Edited by Chic Cicero and Sandra Tabatha Cicero. St. Paul, MN: Llewellyn Publications, 1995.

Wang, Robert. *The Qabalistic Tarot: A Textbook of Mystical Philosophy*. Columbia, MD: Marcus Aurelius Press, 2004.

Magic, Symbolism, Ritual Praxis, and Additional Correspondences (aka "What to Do After Chapter 8")

If, like me, you find yourself unable to stop thinking about the magical implications of tarot once you've gotten the hang of divination, it's time to try and navigate the vast world of contemporary esoteric praxis.

My own journey into magic has been informed by ancestor reverence traditions, the *Greek Magical Papyri* and *Orphic Hymns*, medieval/Renaissance image magic, Jungian psychology, explorations in hoodoo/rootwork, core shamanism, and chaos magick, for a start. My favorite grimoires are the eleventh-century *Picatrix* (or *Ghayat al-Hakim*), Book 2 of Agrippa's *Three Books of Philosophy*, and Book 3 of Marsilio Ficino's *Three Books on Life*. It's a hopelessly spotty hodgepodge of influences; I don't apologize for that because I think it's typical of most magicians' experience.

Your way in will certainly differ, and that's okay. I offer the following list drawn from my own erratic trek across the occult landscape in the hopes that some of the titles may send you down further wormholes that fascinate and inspire you.

Agrippa, Henry Cornelius. *Three Books of Occult Philosophy*. Edited by Donald Tyson. Translated by James Freake. St. Paul, MN: Llewellyn Publications, 2006.

Agrippa, Heinrich Cornelius. *Three Books of Occult Philosophy*. Translated by Eric Purdue. Rochester, VT: Inner Traditions, 2021.

Athanassakis, Apostolos N., and Benjamin M. Wolkow, trans. *The Orphic Hymns*. Baltimore, MD: Johns Hopkins University Press, 2013. (Includes historical commentary.)

Attrell, Dan, and David Porreca, trans. *Picatrix: A Medieval Treatise on Astral Magic*. University Park: Penn State University Press, 2019.

Bills, Rex E. *The Rulership Book: A Directory of Astrological Correspondences*. Tempe, AZ: American Federation of Astrologers, 1991.

Carroll, Peter J. *Liber Null and Psychonaut: The Practice of Chaos Magic*. Newburyport, MA: Weiser Books, 1987.

Chevalier, Jean, and Alain Gheerbrant, eds. *The Penguin Dictionary of Symbols*. Translated by John Buchanan-Brown. New York: Penguin Books, 2008.

Coppock, Austin, and Daniel A. Schulke, eds. *The Celestial Art: Essays on Astrological Magic*. Hercules, CA: Three Hands Press, 2018.

Crowley, Aleister. *777 and Other Qabalistic Writings of Aleister Crowley: Including Gematria & Sepher Sephiroth*. Edited by Israel Regardie. York Beach, ME: Weiser Books, 1996.

Cunningham, Scott. *Cunningham's Encyclopedia of Magical Herbs*. Rev. ed. Woodbury, MN: Llewellyn Publications, 2016.

Dominguez, Ivo. *Keys to Perception: A Practical Guide to Psychic Development*. Newburyport, MA: Weiser Books, 2017.

Dunn, Patrick, trans. *The Orphic Hymns: A New Translation for the Occult Practitioner*. Woodbury, MN: Llewellyn Publications, 2018. (Includes facing-page original text.)

Ficino, Marsilio. *Three Books on Life: A Critical Edition and Translation*. Edited by Carol V. Kaske. Tempe: Arizona Center for Medieval and Renaissance Studies, 2019.

Greer, John Michael, and Christopher Warnock. *The Complete Picatrix: The Occult Classic of Astrological Magic*. Iowa City, IA: Adocentyn Press, 2011.

Hall, Manly P. *The Secret Teachings of All Ages: An Encyclopedic Outline of Masonic, Hermetic, Qabbalistic, and Rosicrucian Symbolical Philosophy*. Seattle: Pacific Publishing Studio, 2011.

Hulse, David Allen. *The Eastern Mysteries: An Encyclopedic Guide to the Sacred Languages & Magickal Systems of the World*. St. Paul, MN: Llewellyn Publications, 2002.

———. *The Western Mysteries: An Encyclopedic Guide to the Sacred Languages & Magickal Systems of the World*. St. Paul, MN: Llewellyn Publications , 2002.

Jung, C. G. "Foreword." *The I Ching or Book of Changes*, translated by Wilhelm/Baynes, xxi–xxxix. Princeton, NJ: Princeton University Press, 1997.

———. *Synchronicity: An Acausal Connecting Principle*. Translated by R. F. C. Hull. Princeton, NJ: Princeton University Press, 2012.

Kraig, Donald Michael. *Tarot & Magic*. St. Paul, MN: Llewellyn Publications, 2003.

Miller, Richard Alan, and Iona Miller. *The Magical and Ritual Use of Perfumes*. Rochester, VT: Destiny Books, 1990.

Moore, Alan, and J. H. Williams. *Promethea*. London: Titan Books, 2003.

Regardie, Israel. *The Golden Dawn: The Original Account of the Teachings, Rites, and Ceremonies of the Hermetic Order*. Edited by John Michael Greer. Woodbury, MN: Llewellyn Publications, 2015.

Skinner, Stephen. *The Complete Magician's Tables*. Singapore: The Golden Hoard Press, 2017.

Steinbrecher, Edwin C. *The Inner Guide Meditation: A Spiritual Technology for the 21st Century*. York Beach, ME: Samuel Weiser, 1988.

von Franz, Marie-Louise. *On Divination and Synchronicity: The Psychology of Meaningful Chance*. Toronto, ON: Inner City Books, 1980.

Wachter, Aidan. *Six Ways: Approaches & Entries for Practical Magic*. Self-pub: Red Temple Press, 2018.

Warnock, Christopher. *Secrets of Planetary Magic*. Self-pub: Renaissance Astrology, 2010.

Whitcomb, Bill. *The Magician's Companion: A Practical & Encyclopedic Guide to Magical & Religious Symbolism*. St. Paul, MN: Llewellyn Publications, 2007.

A Very Incomplete List of Magic-Adjacent Podcasts in Vogue at the Time of This Writing

- *Arnemancy* with Erik Arneson
- *The Astrology Podcast* with Chris Brennan
- *Coffee & Divination* with JoAnna Farrer
- *Fortune's Wheelhouse* with T. Susan Chang and M. M. Meleen
- *Glitch Bottle* with Alexander Eth
- *The Hermit's Lamp* with Andrew McGregor
- *Holes to Heavens* with Adam Sommer
- *The Magician and the Fool* with Dom and Janus
- *Occult Experiments in the Home* with Duncan Barford
- *Rune Soup* with Gordon White
- *This Jungian Life* with Lisa Marchiano, Deb Stewart, and Joseph Lee

NOTES

NOTES

NOTES

NOTES

NOTES